George Saintsbury

A382P 7.5

перг. 15.—

CORRECTED IMPRESSIONS

ESSAYS ON VICTORIAN WRITERS
BY GEORGE SAINTSBURY . . .

NEW YORK: PUBLISHED BY
DODD, MEAD AND COMPANY
MDCCCXCIX

University Press:

John Wilson and Son, Cambridge, U.S.A.

PREFACE.

———◆———

THESE Critical Notes differ a little in
scheme and aim from anything that
their writer has hitherto attempted. The shape
which they take was partly suggested, as is
observed in one of them, by some remarks of
Mr. A. J. Balfour's at the Literary Fund Dinner
of 1893, in London. It occurred to me then
that a kind of foreshortened review of the impressions, and the corrections of them, which
the great Victorian writers had produced or
undergone in my own case during the last thirty
years might not be an absolutely uninteresting
sample of "how it has struck a contemporary."
It was not practically possible to execute this

without some reference to the progress of general as well as of individual opinion. But care has been taken to maintain as far as possible the genuineness of the individual impression, past as well as present. To do this it was necessary rather to give heads of a study of the authors than the completed study itself, and rather to say too little than to say too much; but at the same time not to refrain from a certain amount of personal detail. Some of the earlier papers have appeared in the *Indian Daily News*, and the four last in the New York *Critic*; but none have been printed in England.

G. S.

CONTENTS.

CORRECTED IMPRESSIONS.

I.

THACKERAY.

IN a certain now rather antiquated school of
theology, the word "use" was employed
with a special application, denoting the adjust-
ment of a given text, fact, or other thing to
beneficent moral purposes. I like to make a
use of critical humility out of the fact that there
was a time when I did not like Thackeray. It
was a very short time in itself, and it was a very
long time ago; but from about, so far as I can
remember, my fifteenth year to my seventeenth,
it existed. The circumstances were extenuat-
ing. It so happened that, almost ever since I
could read, I had been brought up on Dickens,
and had known little or nothing of his great
rival in the English fiction of the middle of the
century, except that he was his rival. I believe

the first thing that I ever read of Mr. Thackeray's
was "Philip," as it came out in the *Cornhill;*
the next, "Vanity Fair." Neither, it will probably be admitted, was the best possible introduc-
tion to the subject for a green taste. I now
think considerably better of "Philip" than
some professed Thackerayans do; but I should
hardly quarrel very fiercely with anybody who
failed to relish it. And I do not think that
any boy — at least any boy who is genuine,
and has not prematurely learnt to feign liking
for what he thinks he ought to like — can
really enjoy "Vanity Fair." The full beauty
of Becky (I can honestly say that I always
saw some of it) is necessarily hidden from
him ; he cannot taste the majesty of the
crowning scene with Lord Steyne, or the even
finer, though less dramatic, negotiations which
avert the duel; his knowledge of life is insuffi-
cient to allow him to detect the magnificent
thoroughness and the more magnificent irony
of the general treatment. On the other hand,
he is sure, if he is good for anything, to be
disgusted with the namby-pambyness of Amelia,

with the chuckle-headed goodness of Dobbin, with the vicious nincompoopery and the selfishness of George Osborne. For these are things which, though experience may lead to the retractation of an opinion that any of the three is unnatural, leave on some tolerably mature judgments the impression that they are one-sided and out of composition, if not of drawing.

But this could not last long: after a few months, "Pendennis" came in my way. I took it, I remember very well after thirty years, out of a certain school library, and I read it, or began to read it (an exceedingly reprehensible practice) on my way home, which lay through Hyde Park and Kensington Gardens. If any of the persons into whose arms I walked are still alive, I humbly ask their pardon. Even if they had not now mostly been changed long ago for others, it would be superfluous to extend forgiveness to the Park seats which avenged these innocents on my own knees. It may to some people seem odd, and to others shocking, that "The Newcomes" threw me at first rather back. It had its revenge later,

though. To this day I confess that I think
Ethel rather shadowy, and not wholly attractive;
Clive something of what his own day would
have called a young tiger; and the Colonel himself, despite his angelic qualities and immortal
end, now and then (it is dreadful, but it must
be said) a very little silly.   But "Esmond"
and "The Virginians" together, with their incomparable picture of Beatrix, — the only true
picture of a woman conceived in nature and
sublimed to the seventh heaven by art, in
youth and age alike, that prose fiction contains, — made me live Mr. Thackeray's Pro-
testant to be.   All my old prejudices vanished.
"The wreck was total," as a celebrated epitaph
of the last century has it.   "There was no mistake about this fellow," to alter slightly a great
phrase in one of the novelist's own very best
scenes.

But when you have thus "got salvation" in
matters literary, you do not, if the gods have
made you at all critical, proceed to mere indiscriminate adoring. What you do proceed to
is reading, at first indiscriminate, then tolerably

discriminating, and to the enjoyment of analysing excellence, never without the possibility of admitting defect, but with a sure consciousness that the man you study is right in the main, and that it will be only in a way for his greater glory if you find out where and wherefore he is sometimes wrong. I shall endeavour to set out the chief results of thirty years' reading and rereading of the books of Thackeray in this spirit, only mentioning further, in the same personal key, that, if there is one scene which finally made me his, it is that — slightly done in appearance, and left to produce its own effect, with the carelessness of supremacy — in which Harry Warrington fails to recognise the portrait of Beatrix. If it is not necessary to have read most of the good novels, I would fain persuade myself that it is not unhelpful to have read vast numbers of the bad, in order to see the grandeur of this. America, Russia, France (putting Flaubert out of the question), for thirty years and more, have been trying to beat Thackeray's record in this particular field, and they have never come anywhere near him.

To the corrupted modern man, what other
people say of his subject always has a good
deal to do with his impressions of it, though, if
he be critically given, he can generally get rid
of any bad effect thereof. He takes account
of the sayings, is rather grateful for them, owes
to them sometimes certain initial points of view
and lines of approach, but is not, strictly speaking, much biassed by them. What other people
have said about Thackeray has gone through
some three or four stages. There was the first,
in which they gradually had him forced on their
notice, as a man who wrote a good deal for the
papers. Some, as we learn from the "Life of
Lever," thought he wrote for too many papers,
and was not careful enough in his selection of
those organs. Others, as we learn from a note
to Lockhart's article on "Hook," and those the
acutest judges of the day, thought him a very
remarkable person indeed. He had almost
reached the last decade of his too short life
before this opinion, or conflict of opinion,
changed, — though it must always be remembered that these stages of critical opinion do not

end each as the other begins, but overlap and interpenetrate one another. He was now recognised as one of the greatest writers and one of the greatest novelists of England; he had an ever wider and stronger influence on the coming generation of novelists and of writers; but it was said that he was dreadfully cynical. This stage too passed, at least as a prevailing and recognised stage, and he entered (as most men do who die comparatively young) by the gates of death into something like a full enjoyment of the fame which was his due. Of late years, I am told, and I can partly perceive evidences of it, he has entered yet another phase. His manner, his language, his atmosphere of society, are getting a little antiquated for younger readers. Some critics have persuaded themselves that they see more points in the human soul than he did; his analysis is not quite thorough-going enough, and so forth. Augustus Z. from New York, and M. Jules from Paris (or Quimper), and Count Caviarovitch from Ostrolenko, have outstripped Mr. William Makepeace. He is a little *rococo*.

Let us register these things, and all things.
Perhaps, though it may seem an undue mag-
nification of the critical office, it is never impossible for a competent critic to disentangle
himself almost wholly from prejudices of all
kinds, and to see his subjects, whether they be
subjects two thousand years old, or subjects
of yesterday, or subjects of to-day, in a fairly
white light. The worst of it is that it is so very
difficult to decide what other persons will agree
to regard as a white light. If their own eye-
pieces are not quite achromatic, the whitest light
will seem to them coloured, and they will com-
plain to that effect. But this difficulty has to
be faced.

Of few writers can it be said with so much
confidence as of Thackeray, that he is all of a
piece. He wrote, as has been observed, at one
time of his life rather miscellaneously, and a
great deal of his miscellaneous writing has been
preserved. He was a reviewer of all sorts of
books, a satiric essayist, a literary critic on the
great scale, a social historian, a lecturer, and
a novelist. When he was a novelist, he was

very generally all the other things which have been enumerated at the same time ; and it not unfrequently happened that, in the discharge of his miscellaneous functions, he forgot the particular jacket he had on, and wrote in a character suitable to quite other garments. In "The English Humourists," for instance, and the "Roundabout Papers," he is everything by turns ; and there is hardly one of his novels, from the immaturity of "Catherine" to the uncompleted promise of "Denis Duval," in which the reader who reads with his eyes open does not perceive that he has something much more than a mere novelist to deal with. Not that Thackeray was not a novelist first of all, for if there is one of the pretty numerous gifts which go to make up the novelist which is more indispensable to him than any other, it is the gift of conceiving and projecting character. And this was the essence, the centre, the mainspring, of Thackeray's genius. Whether it was, as a gift, separable from his other peculiar gift of style, is a very intricate question of criticism. But I think the style might have existed without it, and therefore is less distinc-

tive.   Alone among our novelists, if not among
the novelists of the world, Thackeray simply
could not introduce a personage, no matter how
subordinate, without making him a living crea-
ture.   He (or she) may be the central figure of
a long and complicated novel, or may be intro-
duced to say a couple of lines, and never appear
again, but Thackeray has no sooner touched
him than there is a human being,— an entity.
Everybody knows the penalty which is said, in
strict Mohammedan theology, to wait upon the
rash men of art, that they will have somehow or
other to find souls for their creations at the Day
of Judgment, or it will go uncommonly ill with
them.   The prospect must be rather an alarming
one for most "makers" of any kind.   It need
never have troubled Thackeray.   He had done
it beforehand.   He could not introduce a footman, saying some half dozen words, "My Lady
is gone to Bright*ing*," or something of that sort,
without presenting the fellow for his trouble with
life and immortality.

II.

THACKERAY (*concluded*).

IT is perhaps worth while to expand a little
that general view of Thackeray's literary
gifts which has been put above. It must be
remembered that his literary history is decidedly peculiar. He died (as men go) young;
and he began regular — not merely casual or
amateur — literary composition very young indeed. He had dabbled in journalism at Cambridge, and there was not I think any time after
his undergraduate period at which he did not
more or less practise it. Yet he was getting
on for his fortieth year when "Vanity Fair" in
its complete form for the first time forced him
upon the notice of the public as a person who
could not be any longer neglected. Of course,
looking backwards, we think nowadays that
we can detect the excellence which the world
then first recognised in much earlier pieces.

The maddening practice of republishing works in collected editions without giving their original dates (a practice for which, if I were dictator, I would saw any editor or publisher through between two boards) makes it not always easy without elaborate researches to " place " his earlier works exactly. But he certainly had a good ten years' practice in regular harness to all sorts of vehicles, before in 1846 the first instalments of "Vanity Fair" proclaimed him as beyond all doubt or question a master.

There are few more interesting things than to survey all this early work,— the Tales, the Burlesques, the Christmas Stories, the Reviews, the Sketch Books, the what not. It is excessively difficult to decide whether it is real critical acumen or *ex post facto* wiseacre-ishness which makes one fancy that it is possible to detect the true Thackeray even in the very earliest period of the novitiate. But I do not think that I myself ever read a single volume with greater interest than that which I felt in the supplement to his collected works published more than twenty years after his death under the title of " Miscellaneous Essays, etc." It was not that there was anything exactly new in it, for probably all the faults and certainly all the merits could have been paralleled from the work previously issued with the author's own *reimprimatur*. But these were scattered in different volumes. Here they were all in juxtaposition; and as these papers are "impressions," it is not impertinent to add that the time of their appearance was particularly interesting as correcting and strengthening my own notions of Thackeray.

It so happened that for other purposes I had just been refreshing and extending my knowledge of the journalism and magazine work which immediately preceded or accompanied this similar work of his. I had been reading with some care the principal *Blackwood* and *Fraser* men, the latter Thackeray's own colleagues, the former beyond all doubt his and their models. It is only such a comparison and contrast as this which can ever bring out the real and independent value of a new writer. In the course of a good many years' critical reading of literature, I have constantly been struck by this or that trait

in a man only to discover by fuller reading not
so much that he borrowed or plagiarised it from
somebody else (for instances of actual plagiarism
are very rare and as a rule of very little importance) as that it was "in the air" at the time.
But if you compare this miscellaneous work —
originally undistinguished and at all times not
much considered — of Thackeray with the work
of Wilson, of De Quincey, of his own editor
Maginn, and of others, you will very soon begin
to make distinctions and mark advances. There
are of course many likenesses, many copyings
of tricks and mannerisms, many condescendences
of this kind and that. When Thackeray, in a
very sound and agreeable article on " Greenwich
and Whitebait" in *Colburn* for July, 1844, entertained his readers with a procession *nominatim*
of landlords and waiters carrying certain dishes,
he was consciously or unconsciously repeating
an old trick of the " Noctes Ambrosianæ "
which had attained almost to years of discretion as he wrote. But in that very article (one
by no means of his very best) the most careless
reader who can take notice at all will remark

evidences of an "eye on the object," of a
satiric comprehension of life, which is nowhere
in Wilson, nowhere in Maginn, nowhere in De
Quincey, nowhere in their contemporaries, —
which, omitting touches in Scott, had not been
presented in English literature since Fielding.
Such a reader will find too a style which is
strange and new, — not indeed in Thackeray
himself, for touches of it may be found seven
years earlier in his very earliest work, but as
compared with others, — a quiet faculty of saying remarkable things and leaving them to
make their own effect, a sort of urbane ease,
an unforced combination of the points of view
of the man of letters and the man of the world.
And perhaps it may be remembered that Fielding also wandered about in alien paths of literature long before he found his true way, and that
in his Miscellanies also are the strangest antici-
pations and revealings of his future powers.

Although, therefore, these early works, including even the famous "Sketch Books" and such
things as the "Hoggarty Diamond," are amaz-
ingly unequal and contain some things almost

bad, they also contain intrinsic attraction enough to content, I should say, the most uncritical reader who knows good things when he sees them, while for critical attraction I think they positively grow on one.

But there are two ends, according to the proverb, to some if not all subjects; and it is not seldom asked whether there was not a decline as well as a growth of Thackeray's powers, and whether anything but "Vanity Fair," "Pendennis," "The Newcomes," and "Esmond" can be considered to present that power at its height. It is impossible not to observe, in passing, what a genius that must be as to which it is matter of dispute whether anything has to be *added* to such a literary baggage as that of the four books just enumerated. The least of them would be a passport to and a provision for eternity; and we are inquiring whether the gentleman has any more titles and any more luggage than all four. Let me only say that I am more and more convinced that he has: that he has others even besides "The Four Georges," "The English Humourists," and the "Roundabout Papers,"

which even his most grudging critics would in
the same good-natured manner allow. I have
never quite understood the common depreciation of "The Virginians," which contains things
equal, if not superior, to the very finest of its
author's other work, and includes the very
ripest expression of his philosophy of life.
For though indeed I do not approve a novel
more because it contains the expression of a
philosophy of life, others do. So, too, the
irregularity and formlessness of plot which char-
acterised most of Thackeray's work undoubtedly
appear in it; but then, according to the views
of our briskest and most modern critics, plot is
a very subordinate requisite in a novel, and may
be very well dispensed with. Here again I do
not agree, and I should say that Thackeray's
greatest fault was his extreme inattention to
construction, which is all the more remarkable
inasmuch as he was by no means a very rapid
or an extremely prolific writer. But if both
these faults were infinitely greater than they are,
I should say that the perfect command of character and the extraordinary criticisms of life

2

which "The Virginians" contains save it, and not merely save it, but place it far above almost everything outside its writer's own work.

"Lovel the Widower," amusing as it is, falls admittedly on a lower plane, and I do not know that its earlier dramatic form, "The Wolves and the Lamb," is not its superior. But "Philip" is, I believe, the great stumbling-block. I have owned that it was so to me in my green, unknowing youth. Nor in a rather gray and at least partially knowing age could I attempt to put it on a level with the others, despite a crowd of admirable scenes and incidents. Sometimes I have thought that Thackeray's infallible eye for life played him a trick from which less alert and more blear-eyed talents were free. His own generation was passing, but he could not help catching something of the way of the generation that was growing up. The consequence is that the manners and speech of Philip here are as bewildering as the actual chronology, — which refers to Mr. Anthony Trollope as an object of the hero's admiration at a time when, comparing other things, it is certain that Mr.

Trollope had not even made his first literary
ventures. Philip is neither a young man of
1830 nor a young man of 1860, nor, as Arthur
Pendennis and Henry Esmond are in their different ways, a young man of all time adjusted to
a particular date. He is neither one thing nor
the other. And when he talks about " the kids
and Char," I could almost call him — but what
I could almost call him is too terrible to put to
paper.

Yet even of this book, the most dubious of
the later, as of " Catherine," the most dubious
of the earlier, we may say, Who but Thackeray
could have written it? and, even after thirty
years' reading, How shall we be grateful enough
to Thackeray for having written it? For here,
as nowhere else except in Fielding himself, is a
world of fictitious personages who are all alive,
who cannot, for the very life of them, say or do
anything unnatural. Why that should be per-
manently charming in art which is frequently
tedious in nature is hard, is perhaps impossible
to tell, and certainly there is no need to discuss
the question here. But the fact is a fact beyond

question, and it is in this fact mainly that the
certainty of Thackeray's appeal consists. A
favourable impression of him, once reached,
whether by happy chance or sufficient study, is
a *ne varietur*, never more to be corrected or
altered.

III.

TENNYSON.

AT the Literary Fund dinner of 1893 Mr.
Arthur Balfour, in an unusually interesting
speech for that occasion, hinted that he was not
himself able to take quite so much pleasure in
what is called Victorian Literature — the literature of which the late Lord Tennyson in verse,
and Mr. Carlyle in prose, were the unquestioned
chiefs — as some other persons appeared to do.
He suggested that this might have been due to
his being born a little too late. If the cause
assigned is a *vera causa*, it is one of some interest to me. For I happen to have been born not
quite three years before Mr. Balfour, and therefore I ought to have been exposed to very much
the same "skiey influences" in point of time.

Yet I do not think that any one can ever
have had and maintained a greater admiration
for the author of "The Lotos-Eaters" than I

have. This admiration was born early, but it
was not born full grown. I am so old a Tennysonian that though I can only vaguely remember talk about " Maud " at the time of its first
appearance, I can remember the " Idylls " themselves fresh from the press. I was, however, a
little young then to appreciate Tennyson, and it
must have been a year or two later that I began
to be fanatical on the subject. Yet there must
have been a little method in that youthful mad-
ness, — some criticism in that craze. A great
many years afterwards I came across the decla-
ration of Edward Fitzgerald, one of the poet's
oldest and fastest friends, to the effect that
everything he had written after 1842 was a
falling off. That of course was a crotchet.
Fitzgerald, like all men of original but not very
productive genius who live much alone, was a
crotcheteer to the nth. But it has a certain
root of truth in it; and as I read it I remembered what my own feelings had been on reading " Enoch Arden," the first volume that came
out after I had enrolled myself in the sacred
band. It was just at the end of my fresh-

man's year; and I bought a copy of the book (for which there had been some waiting, and a tremendous rush) on my way home from the prize-giving of my old school. To tell the truth, I was a little disappointed. For "Enoch Arden" itself, as a whole, I have never cared, despite the one splendid passage describing the waiting in the island; nor for "Aylmer's Field"; nor for divers other things. "The Voyage" was of the very best, and "In the Valley at Canterets," and one or two other things. "Boadicea" was an interesting experiment. But on the whole one was inclined to say, Where is "The Lo-tos-Eaters"? Where is the "Dream of Fair Women"? Where is "The Palace of Art"?

Perhaps they were nowhere; perhaps only in the very best things of the "Ballads" of 1880, and one or two later, did the poet ever touch the highest points of his first fine raptures. But he never failed, even to his death day, to show that he was the author of these raptures, and that he could still go very near, if not absolutely up to them, when he chose. It has, however, been a constant critical amusement of mine to try to find out if possible whether this impression was a mere fallacy of youth, and if so how far. And some of the results of the inquiry which has been going on more or less ever since I turned through the Marble Arch into Hyde Park, and took "Enoch Arden" out of my pocket on that summer day, may not improperly form the subject of this and another of these papers. For the inevitable *post-mortem* depreciation has set in in reference to this great poet already, and it may not be uninteresting to others to see how it strikes a contemporary who had prepared himself for it.

Readers, and I hope they are many, of Maginn's "Story without a Tail" will remember the various reasons assigned for taking a dram, until the candid narrator avowed that he took it "because he liked a dram." It is undoubtedly natural to humanity to disguise to itself the reasons and nature of its enjoyments; but I do not know that it exhibits this possibly amiable and certainly amusing weakness more curiously or more distinctly in any matter than in the matter of poetry. Men will try to persuade

themselves, or at least others, that they read
poetry because it is a criticism of life, because
it expresses the doubts and fears and thoughts
and hopes of the time, because it is a substitute
for religion, because it is a relief from serious
work, because and because and because. As a
matter of fact, they (that is to say those of them
who like it genuinely) read it because they like
it, because it communicates an experience of
half-sensual, half-intellectual pleasure to them.
Why it does this no mortal can say, any more
than he can say why the other causes of his
pleasures produce their effect. *How* it does, it
is perhaps not quite so hard to explain; though
here also we come as usual to the bounding-wall
of mystery before very long. And it is further
curious to note that the same kind of prudery
and want of frankness comes in here once more.
It often makes people positively angry to be
told that the greatest part, if not the whole, of
the pleasure-giving appeal of poetry lies in its
sound rather than in its sense, or, to speak with
extreme exactness, lies in the manner in which
the sound conveys the sense. No " chain of ex-

tremely valuable thoughts " is poetry in itself: it only becomes poetry when it is conveyed with those charms of language, metre, rhyme, cadence, what not, which certain persons disdain.

This being so, and the mere matter of all poetry — to wit, the appearances of nature and the thoughts and feelings of man — being unalterable, it follows that the difference between poet and poet will depend upon the manner of each in applying language, metre, rhyme, cadence, and what not to this invariable material. If the poet follows some one else's manner, he may be agreeable, but will not be great; if he is great, he will have a distinctly new and original manner of his own. It sometimes happens, too, that he will have a manner so new and so original that his time will be at first deaf to it. We have all heard of the strange objections which even Coleridge, who might have been thought most likely of all living men to appreciate Tennyson, made (though he did not fail wholly in his appreciation) to the new poet's manner. I knew a much lesser but even more curious and far more recent instance myself.

A boy of eighteen or nineteen, altogether average except that he had, I think, some Eurasian strain in him, neither a dunce nor a genius and decidedly fond of reading, once took out of a library the "Poems," — *the* "Poems," that is to say the volume containing everything before the "Idylls" except "Maud," "The Princess," and "In Memoriam." After a day or so he returned it, saying sadly to the librarian that "he could not read it. It was just like prose." Had he been Dr. Johnson he would probably have said that "the rhymes were harsh and the numbers unpleasing," just as the Doctor did of "Lycidas."

To us, of course, on the other hand, the whole or the greatest charm of Tennyson comes from the fact that he affects us in exactly the opposite way. But I think there is a certain excuse for the laughers of 1830, for Coleridge, and for my Eurasian schoolfellow. I am sure at least that I myself read Tennyson and liked him (for I always liked him) for several years before his peculiar and divine virtue dawned upon me. It has never set or paled since, and I am as sure

as I can be that if I were to live to be a Struld-
brug (which Heaven forbid) one of the very
last things of the kind that I should forget or
lose my relish for would be this. But comparatively few people, I think, have ever fully recog-
nized how extremely original this virtue of his
is. The word " great " is most irritatingly mis-
used about poets; and we have quite recently
found some persons saying that " Tennyson is
as great as Shakespeare," and other people
going into fits of wrath, or smiling surprise with
calm disdain, at the saying. If what the former
mean to say and what the latter deny is that
Tennyson has a supreme and peculiar poetic
charm, then I am with the former and against
the latter. He has: and from the very fact of
his having it he will not necessarily be appreciated at once, and may miss appreciation
altogether with some people.

The recent publication anew of the earliest
" Poems by Two Brothers " has been especially
useful in enabling us to study this charm. In
these poems it is absolutely nowhere: there is
not from beginning to end in any verse, whether

attributed to Alfred, Frederick, or Charles, one suggestion even of the witchery that we Tennysonians associate with the work of the first-named. It appears dimly and distantly — so dimly and distantly that one has to doubt whether we recognise it by anything but a "fallacy of looking back" — in "Timbuctoo," in "The Lovers' Tale" quite distinctly, but uncertainly; and with much alloy in the pieces which the author later labelled as "Juvenilia."

It is true that these "Juvenilia" have been a good deal retouched, and that much of the really juvenile work on which the critics were by no means unjustly severe has been left out. But the charm is there. Take the very first stanza of "Claribel." You may pick holes in the conceit which makes a verb "I low-lie, thou low-liest, she low-lieth," and you may do other things of the same kind if you like. But who ever wrote like that before? Who struck that key earlier? Who produced anything like the slow, dreamy music of the variations in it? Spenser and Keats were the only two masters of anything in the remotest degree similar in

English before.   And yet it is perfectly independent of Spenser, perfectly independent of
Keats.   It is Tennyson, the first rustle of the
" thick-leaved, ambrosial " murmuring which was
to raise round English lovers of poetry a very
Broceliande of poetical enchantment for sixty
years to come during the poet's life, and after
his death for as long as books can speak and
readers hear.

IV.

TENNYSON (*concluded*).

I BELIEVE that, in so far as the secret of a poet can be discovered and isolated, the secret of Tennyson lies in that slow and dreamy music which was noticed at the end of the last paper; and I am nearly sure that my own admiration of him dates from the time when I first became aware of it. "Claribel," of course, is by no means a very effective example; though the fact of its standing in the very forefront of the whole work is excessively interesting. The same music continued to sound — with infinite variety of detail, but with no breach of general character — from "Claribel" itself to "Crossing the Bar." At no time was Tennyson a perfect master of the quick and lively measures; and in comparison he very seldom affected them. He cannot pick up and return the ball of song as Praed — another great master

of metre if not quite of music, who preceded
him by seven years at Trinity — did, still less
as Praed partly taught Mr. Swinburne to do.
There is nothing in Tennyson of the hurrying
yet never scurrying metre of "At a Month's
End," or the Dedication to Sir Richard Burton.
His difficulty in this respect has not improved
"The Charge of the Light Brigade," and it is
noticeable that it impresses a somewhat grave
and leisurely character even on his anapæsts, —
as for instance in the "Voyage of Maeldune."
If you want quick music you must go elsewhere, or be content to find the poet not at his
best in it.

But in the other mode of linked and long-
drawn out sweetness he has hardly any single
master and no superior :

> *"At midnight the moon cometh*
> *And looketh down alone."*

There again the despised "Claribel" gives
us the cue. And how soon and how miracu-
lously it was taken up, sustained, developed, varied, everybody who knows Tennyson knows.

"Mariana" is the very incarnation, the very embodiment in verse of spell-bound stagnation, that is yet in the rendering beautiful. The "Recollections of the Arabian Nights" move something sprightlier, but the "Ode to Memory," by far the greatest of the "Juvenilia," relapses into the visionary gliding. Even in "The Sea Fairies" and "The Dying Swan," the occasional dactyls and anapæsts rather slide than skip; and the same is the case with the best lines in "Oriana" and (naturally enough) with the whole course of the "Dirge." All the ideal girl-portraits except "Lilian" (the least worthy of them) have this golden languor, which is so distinctly the note of the earlier poems that it is astonishing any one should ever have missed it. Yet, as I have said, I believe I missed it myself for some time, and certainly, judging from their criticisms, contemporaries of the poet much cleverer than I never seem to have heard it at all.

When the great collection came it must have been hard still to miss it; yet how little the English public even yet was attuned is shown by the fact that both then and since one of the most popular things has been " The May Queen," which, if anything of Tennyson's could be so, I should myself be disposed to call trumpery. " The Lady of Shalott" is very far from trumpery, and perhaps the poet's very happiest thing not in a languid measure ; but even "The Lady of Shalott " does not count among the poems that established Tennyson's title to the first rank among English poets. " The Lotos-Eaters," " The Palace of Art," "A Dream of Fair Women," " Œnone," " Ulysses," (though perhaps it will be said that I ought not to in-clude blank verse pieces,) all have the trailing garments of the night, not the rush and skip of dawn ; and though there are some exceptions among the rightly famous lyrics, such as " Sir Galahad " and the admirable piece of cynicism in " The Vision of Sin," they are exceptions. Even " Locksley Hall " canters rather than gallops, and the famous verses in " The Brook " are but a *tour de force*.

But it would be impossible here to go through the whole of the poet's work. He can

do many things; but he always (at least to my
taste) does his best in lyric to slow music.
And I doubt whether any one will again produce this peculiar effect as he has produced it.
It must be evident, too, how much this faculty of
slow and stately verse adds to the effect of " In
Memoriam." If the peculiar metre of that
poem is treated (as I have known it treated by
imitators) in a light and jaunty fashion — to
quick time, so to speak — the effect is very
terrible. But Tennyson has another secret than
this for blank verse. This is the secret of the
paragraph, which he alone of all English poets
shares with Milton in perfection. There is little
doubt that he learnt it from Milton, but the
effect is quite different, though the means re-
sorted to are necessarily much the same in
both cases, and include in both a very careful and deliberate disposition of the full stop
which breaks and varies the cadence of the
line; the adoption when it is thought necessary
of trisyllabic instead of dissyllabic feet; and
the arrangement of a whole block of verses
so that they lead up to a climax of sense and

sound in the final line.   Almost the whole secret
can be found in one of the earliest and perhaps the finest of his blank verse exercises, the
"Morte d'Arthur," but examples were never
wanting up to his very last book.

These two gifts, that of an infinitely varied
slow music and dreamy motion in lyric and
that of concerted blank verse, with his almost
unequalled faculty of observation and phrasing
as regards description of nature, were, I think,
the things in Tennyson which first founded
Tennyson-worship in my case.   And these, I am
sure, are what have kept it alive in my case,
though I have added to them an increasing
appreciation of his wonderful skill in adjusting
vowel values.   His subjects matter little : I do
not know that subject ever does matter much
in poetry, though it is all important in prose.
But if I have been right in my selection of his
chief gifts, it will follow almost as the night the
day that the vague, the antique, and to some
extent the passionate, must suit him better
than the modern, the precise, the meditative.
Not that Tennyson is by any means as some

misguided ones hold, a shallow poet; the exquisite perfection of his phrase and his horror
of jargon have deceived some even of the
elect on that point, just as there have been
those who think that Plato is shallow because
he is nowhere unintelligible, and that Berkeley
cannot be a great philosopher because he is
a great man of letters. But art, romance,
distant history (for history of a certain age
simply becomes romance), certainly suit him
better than science, modern life, or argument.
Vast efforts have been spent on developing
schemes of modernised Christianity out of " In
Memoriam"; but the religious element in that
poem is as consistent with an antiquated ortho-
doxy as with anything new and undogmatic;
and the attraction of the poem is in its human
affection, in its revelation of the House of
Mourning, and above all in those unmatched
landscapes and sketches of which the poet is
everywhere prodigal.

It is perhaps (if I may refine still further on
the corrections of impressions which years of
study have left) in the combination of the faculty

of poetical music with that of poetical picture
drawing that the special virtue of Tennyson lies.
There have been poets, though not many, who
could manage sound with equal skill; and there
have been those, though not many, who could
bring with a few modulated words a visual picture
before the mind's eye and almost the eye of the
body itself with equal sureness and success.
But there have hardly been any, outside the very
greatest Three or Four, who could do both these
things at the same time in so consummate a
fashion. The very musical poets are too apt to
let the sharp and crisp definition of their picture
be washed away in floods of sound; the very
pictorial poets to neglect the musical accompani-
ment. Tennyson never commits either fault.
The wonderful successions of cartoons in the
" Palace " and the " Dream " exhibit this in his
very earliest stage. If any one has ever in this
combination of music, draughtsmanship, and
colour equalled him who wrote,

> " *One seemed all dark and red, a tract of sand,*
> *And some one pacing there alone,*
> *Who paced for ever in a glimmering land,*
> *Lit with a low large moon,*"

I do not know him.   The first stanza of "The Lotos-Eaters" has the same power of filling eye and ear at once, so that it is almost impossible to decide whether you hear the symphony or see the picture most clearly.   And at the very other extreme of the poet's poetical life, in those famous lines which united all competent suffrages (though one egregious person I remember called them "homely" and divers wiseacres puzzled over the identity of the "pilot" and the propriety of his relation of place toward the "bar"), this master faculty again appeared.

> *"With such a tide as moving seems asleep,*
> *Too full for sound or foam,"*

are words which make the very picture, the very foamless swirl, the very soundless volume of sound, which they describe.

No!   In the impressions given by such a poet as this, when they have been once duly and fairly received, there can be no correction, except a better and better appreciation of him as time goes on.   The people who have liked what was not best, or have not liked what was best, may grow weary of well admiring.   Those who look

rather at the absence of faults than at the presence of beauties may point to incongruities and
mediocrities, to attempts in styles for which the
poet had little aptitude, to occasional relapses
from the grand manner to the small mannerism,
and so forth. But those whose ears and eyes
(if not, alas! their lips) Apollo has touched,
will never make any mistake about him. They
may as in other — as in all — cases be more or
fewer as time goes on: there may be seasons
when the general eye grows blind and the general
ear deaf to his music and his vision. But that
will not matter at all. So long as the unknown
laws which govern the presentation of beauty in
sight and sound last, beauty will be discovered
here just as we ourselves after two thousand
years find it in the ancient tongues which we
cannot even pronounce with any certainty that
we are nearer to the original than Mr. Hamer-
ton's little French boy was when he tried to
vocalise that very stanza of "Claribel" to which
I have referred above.

V.

CARLYLE.

I BELIEVE it will be generally admitted that there is nowadays no more distinct sign of a man's having reached the fogey, and of his approaching the fossil, stage of intellectual existence than the fact that he has an ardent admiration for Carlyle. I have collected this inference from a large number of observations; and, if I am not mistaken, have seen it more than once definitely laid down as a starting point and premiss by the younger sort. This is not only interesting in itself, but also and perhaps still more as an instance of the truth of the ancient saying that old age cometh upon a man without his perceiving it. For it was but, so to speak, the other day that to admire Carlyle was still a mark, not indeed of intense or daring innovation (that stage was over when the present writer was in his nurse's arms), but yet of heresy and

opposition to the settled precepts of the sages.
It cannot be said that up to Carlyle's own death
the constituted authorities in things literary and
intellectual were ever fully reconciled to his style,
his thought, or his general attitude; and great
as is the influence which — especially perhaps
during the third quarter of the century — he
exercised over individuals, no party in politics,
no school in letters or philosophy, ever could
claim him or stomach him, as a whole stomachs
a whole.

It is the proudest memory of my own life
that a person of distinction once said to me
in a rage, "You like Carlyle because he has
made you more of a Tory than the Devil had
made you already." But without admitting or
denying the justice of this soft impeachment in
the individual case, it is quite certain that Tories
as a class did *not* like Mr. Carlyle, nor he them.
They did not like him because of his flings and
crotchets on separate parts of their creed; he
did not like them because, I think, he knew
himself to be one of them and yet would not
confess it. The average mid-century Liberal, on

the other hand, could not help — unless he was a very dull or a very clever man indeed — regarding Mr. Carlyle as something like Antichrist, a defender of slavery, a man whose dearest delight it was to gore and toss and trample the sweetest and most sacred principles of the Manchester school; a stentorian scoffer who roared sarcasms over Progress and Perfectibility, and to whom House of Commons, manufacturing centres, Great Exhibitions, and so forth, were only different kinds of filthy and futile bauble shops. It was impossible, I say, that the mid-century Liberal, whether his Liberalism was of the common-sense type of Macaulay, or the doctrinaire type of Mill, or the sentimental type of Dickens, should do anything but regard Carlyle as a kind of hippopotamus, ravaging and trampling the fair fields of promise.

But the curious thing is that no reaction of the usual kind has come to his rescue. The parties, or the names, (for I own that I see uncommonly little difference between Tories and Liberals now,) that represent the modifications of public opinion by the results of the Second and Third Reform Bills, have not gone as a rule nearer to, but farther from Carlyle's ideal. It is impossible to imagine anything more anti-Carlylian than the washy semi-Socialism, half sentimental, half servile, which is the governing spirit of all but a very few politicians to-day. Nor is it surprising that a world which, whether with tongue in cheek or not, praises, blesses, and magnifies "democracy," should be enthusiastic in favour of a prophet whose relation to democracy was pretty exactly the relation of Elijah to Baal. Add to this the existence of a considerable literary class which takes very little interest in politics, a good deal in art (for which Carlyle cared absolutely nothing), and most of all in mere literature (which he always attempted to scorn and snub), and it is not very surprising that Carlyle is not popular nowadays with our youth, and that to admire him is, as I have said, the mark of a fogey and a fossil.

So be it. Yet the fossil is a thing that abides, and has not even Mr. Thackeray sung the joys of being a fogey? At any rate, as for me and my intellectual house, we intend to continue to serve Carlyle. Whether it be due to those pre-

liminary operations of the Devil, to which my
friend referred, or to some other reason, I cannot remember a period at which the reading of
Carlyle was not to me as the reading of something that one had always thought but had never
been able to express. It was a lucky accident,
no doubt, that I began at the beginning, to wit,
with " Sartor Resartus," which I remember reading at so early an age that a great part of it
must have been the merest Abracadabra to me.
But there is nothing like providing children
(accidentally, if possible) with good abracada-
bras which as they grow up shall become clear
to them. If anybody had preached Carlyle to
me, I dare say I should have been much longer
before the honey in that lion won my tongue,
but as it was the process of discovery was sure,
if not excessively rapid. The " Cromwell " did
indeed a little stick in my gizzard until I was
old enough to discover the truth that Carlyle's
particular fads and fancies are, as a rule, matters
of no particular importance, and that his general attitude is the pearl of price. And by
some happy chance the " Latter Day Pam-

phlets" did not come in my way till I had already begun to take a considerable interest in politics. That book, with all its divagations, all its extravagances, all its occasional lapses of taste and unadvised speaking about things which Carlyle miscomprehended, partly owing to education and partly owing to pride, seems to me the very gospel of English politics in modern times, a sort of modern "Politicus" in the spirit and tone of which every Englishman should strive to soak and saturate himself. It seemed to me so then: it has never failed to seem so since.

It is, I think, the mistake of demanding a positive gospel instead of negative warnings in the first place, and in the second the inability to appreciate "the humour of it" to the full, which have been at the root of most recent depreciation of Carlyle, though no doubt also reaction from the violent mannerisms of his style and a not ungenerous but rather unintelligent disgust at the inordinately voluminous and very ill-managed personal revelations of his life must also be allowed for. People have insufficiently appreciated the symbolism which plays so very

large a part in his work. The two largest individual parts of that work are occupied, the one
with an apotheosis from the point of view of a
denouncer of cant of a man who canted against
despotism his way to the headship of the Com-
monwealth of England, and then continued to
cant as a despot to the day of his death, the
other with the glorification of a selfish and sor-
did scoundrel whose chief merits were that he
had an indomitable will, and could have written a
sincere and forcible treatise *De Contemptu Vitæ*.
But, by a paradox which I have never been able
to make up my mind whether to attribute to a
completely or a partially humoristic view, the
Cromwell and the Frederick of Carlyle, though
he has delineated them for the benefit of other
people with a fidelity and a vigour of bio-
graphical art beside which even Boswell, even
Lockhart, are tame and shadowy, are as objects
of admiration pure symbols. The unctuous
butcher of Tredagh, who pretended to revenge
the massacres committed by the Irish of 1641
on a garrison which he knew to consist very
largely of pure English troops, the filibuster of

Silesia and the fribble of Rheinsberg, who had
all vices but those that are amiable and hardly
any virtues but those which are unattractive, live
as they lived in his pages.   Nobody but a mere
idiot can accuse Carlyle of garbling out a damn-
ing or foisting in a flattering trait.   And yet all
the while he is glorifying and extolling in the
one a symbol of upright humanity, in the other
a symbol of patriotic heroism.

These apparent contradictions run throughout
not only these books, but a great part of Carlyle's
other works, and they seem to have been too
much for many.   "Am I to admire a brute like
Frederick?" says, and says not ungenerously,
the neophyte.   "I won't do anything of the
kind!"   And he does not see that what he is
required to admire is — not the actual Frederick
who was a kind of crowned bandit in public life,
and in 'private a harsh master, a fickle friend, a
stingy patron, a man of the worst possible taste
in æsthetics and ethics, spiteful, treacherous,
mean — but a Frederick who is a kind of ab-
straction of the Ruler, a personified and incar-
nate Government.   Indeed, the fact of this being

practically Carlyle's last book, and the only one which he wrote for a very large public, with the further facts of its enormous size, of its being written in a sort of short-hand of mannerism and of its containing besides the panegyric of Frederick himself, the apology at least of his father, must be admitted to have been unfortunate, and to have accounted to some extent for that sudden falling off of Carlylians which has been noted. For it so happened that the very generation which in the natural course of things grew up prepared to be his admirers was, to speak vernacularly, choked off by the issue of this huge and not altogether grateful history for years running. No book probably could be worse to begin a study of Carlyle upon.

And this, I think, is a pretty full account of the various adverse influences to which the Carlylian impressions of a man who began Carlyle, as I did, thirty or five and thirty years ago, have been exposed in the mean time. It will take another paper to say something of the effect, whether of correction or confirmation, that they have undergone in consequence.

4

VI.

CARLYLE (*concluded*).

IT will perhaps have appeared already from
what was said in the last paper that, after
having passed through, or at least been contemporary with, all the fluxes and gusts of opinion there mentioned, I am an impenitent and
hardened Carlylian. Of course a great deal has
to be added to Carlyle, and, as has been already
admitted and asserted, something has to be
taken away from him—in the sense that no man
in his senses would attempt to indorse every
particular Carlylian utterance. He was often
bilious; he was not seldom blind; and as for his
strange contemporary and counterpart across
the Channel, who for half a dozen years less at
the beginning, and half a dozen more at the
end, represented the French genius just as
Carlyle did the English, it was almost impossible for him not to caricature and reduce to the

absurd his own views and formulas, though he and Victor Hugo achieved this result in very different ways. The Carlylians pure and simple, though they included some men of genius such as were at different times Kingsley and Mr. Ruskin and Mr. Froude, were apt to be rather terrible as well as brilliant examples. When they were not brilliant they were terrible purely. They are not very rampant now, and it would be unkind to specify them by name; but it may be most frankly confessed that "middle-class Carlylese" was one of the worst dialects ever known, both in form and in matter.

Indeed, there are not inconsiderable regions of interest where Carlyle does not count. For the whole domain of the plastic arts he seems to have had no kind of fancy or faculty. Even in literature, though at his best and in his earlier days, when he had not begun to "pontify" and in the solitude of Craigenputtock took real trouble to master his subjects, he attained the very first rank as a literary critic, there were large gaps and rents in his faculty of appreciation. He seems to have wanted — a want which

I fear is more common than is allowed to appear
— all affection, all sense of any kind for poetry
as poetry. Some of the greatest expression on
things which he did care for is to be found in
poets, and then he cared for them; but it was
not as poets. The same exactly may be said of
his attitude to prose fiction. Except on the
purely mathematical side, he did not, I think
care much for science. For all forms of theology he had a disdain which was partly igno-
rant and a mere expression of personal distaste,
partly I fear a form of personal arrogance. In
philosophy itself I do not know that he was very
great on the purely metaphysical side. But, like
Henry the Eighth, he "loved a man," and I am
not quite sure that (in this respect not resem-
bling that sovereign) he qualified the affection
by any others. Such a historian on the bio-
graphical and anthropological side the world
has never seen. To his own contemporaries he
was often foolishly and scandalously unjust;
and probably nothing has done him so much
harm with those who are apt to fly off at tan-
gents when special points of their own fancy are

touched, as his posthumous depreciations of
Lamb, of De Quincey, of Newman, and of others as different in their different ways as these.
But when he got hold of "a man" in history, it
seems to me that it was absolutely impossible
for him to miss hitting off that man to the life.
And he could in the same way seize a period, a
movement, a set of incidents, with a grasp of
which I am sure it is enough, and I do not think
that it is too much, to say that the result was
Gibbon without his obstinate superficiality, and
Thucydides without his disappointing asceticism
in rhetoric and eloquence.

Take, for instance, "The French Revolution."
It has been to me an inexhaustible joy for twenty
or thirty years past to read the excellent persons who, in English and French and German,
have undertaken to "correct" Carlyle. They
have demonstrated in I dare say the most sufficient and triumphant way that he sometimes
represents a thing as having happened at two
o'clock on Thursday when it actually happened on Tuesday at three o'clock. They
have, I believe, made some serious emenda-

tions in the number of leagues travelled and
the *menu* of the meals eaten by Louis the Six-
teenth on his way to and from Varennes. But
have they to the satisfaction of the *phronimos*,
the Aristotelian intelligent person, altered or
destroyed one feature in the Carlylian picture
of the uprising and of the Terror? Not they.
On the contrary, the greatest of them all, M.
Taine, after protesting against Carlyle in his
youth came to tread in Carlyle's very steps in
his age. And it could not be otherwise. The
French Revolution of Carlyle is the French
Revolution as it happened, as it was. The
French Revolution of the others is the French
Revolution dug up in lifeless fragments by
excellent persons with the newest patent pick-
axes. I do not know whether this extraordinary
historico-biographical faculty can be in any way
connected, after the fashion of cause and effect,
with his other great quality, his peculiar way of
treating ethics and politics, the only subjects in
which he seems to have taken a thorough interest. Man to him was indeed a " political beast "
in the old phrase, extending the meaning to eth-

ics as the Greeks themselves would have done.
Here again there were no doubt gaps, especially
that huge one of his complete incapacity to
enter into the very important division of human
sentiment, which is called for shortness love.
Of "the way of a man with a maid" Carlyle
never showed much comprehension, nor in it
much interest, which is doubtless a pity. But of
the way of a man in political society he showed
a very great comprehension indeed, as well as of
that other way which his forefathers would have
called "walking with God," that is to say, of personal conduct and attitude towards the fortunes
and mysteries of life.

It is here that his gift of many-coloured and
many-formed language was applied most remarkably and perhaps most profitably. As has
been said, or hinted, above, it is not to Carlyle
that you must go for positive precepts of any
kind. But as a negative teacher he has few
equals. "Don't funk; don't cant; don't gush;
don't whine; don't chatter;" — these and some
others like them were his commandments, and I
do not know where to look for a better set of

their kind. But they were elementary and trivial in reference to certain larger and vaguer precepts of the Carlylian decalogue or myriologue. The two greatest of these, as it seems to me, are, "Never mistake the amount, infinitesimal if not *minus*, of your own personal worth and importance in this world," on the one hand, and "Never care for any majority of other infinitesimals who happen to be against you," on the other. Ever since 1789 at least, the idol from which men should have prayed to be kept, and which has been growing year by year and decade by decade, is the worship of the majority; and the cream, the safest and soundest part of the Carlylian doctrine, is: "Don't care one rap, or the ten-thousandth part of one rap, for the majority. You may be — you very likely are — a fool yourself; but it is as nearly as possible certain that the majority of the majority are fools, and therefore, though you need not necessarily set yourself against them, you are absolutely justified in neglecting them." "Do your duty," which he also preached, is of course a more strictly virtuous doctrine, and it is also a much older one. But it is open to the retort, " Yes, but what is my duty? " which is never specially easy and often extremely difficult to answer. Nor is it more specially suited for this day than for any other. But " Don't worship the majority " is the very commandment needed in the nineteenth century, and likely, it would seem, to be needed still more in the twentieth. Even if, as it rarely may be, the majority is right, the fact that it is the majority does not make it so, and when there is no reason for believing it to be right except that it is the majority, then that is reason sufficient for electing to regard it as wrong.

This anti-democratic tone and temper — enforced and fed, it may be, in his own case, by too much indulgence in the luxury of scorn, by too much contempt for his fellows, by too unsocial a view of life — was, as it seems to me, what Carlyle had to teach and did teach. His applications of it in particular may not always have been wise, but they were made always with the most astonishing *diable au corps*, and in a style which, though I should

be very sorry to see it generally imitated, and
though it was sometimes very nearly bad, was
at its best surpassed by no style, either in English or in any other language, for pure force and
intense effect, — full of lights and colours, now
as fierce as those of fire, now as tender as those
of fire also, — full of voices covering the whole
gamut from storm to whisper. Whether the
great volume of his work, the exceptions, the
inequalities, the crotchets and lacks of catholi-
city in it, will seriously injure that work with
posterity is of course very difficult to say.
Work which requires, as this does, a certain
initiation and novitiate, perhaps also a certain
pre-established harmony of temper and taste,
is always heavily weighted in competing for
the attention of posterity. But I hope at least
that Carlyle will continue even in the evil days
to inspire some with determination *malignum
spernere vulgus ;* and I feel nearly sure that when
the tide turns, as it must some day, and the rule
of the best and fewest, not of the most and worst,
again becomes the favourite, his works will sup-
ply texts for the orthodox as they now do for

heretics. At any rate, I am sure that no one who ever goes to them will miss the splendours of pure literature which illuminate their rugged heights and plateaus, and that some at least will recognize and rejoice in the high air of love for noble things and contempt for things base which sweeps over and through them.

VII.

MR. SWINBURNE.

I DO not suppose that anybody now alive
(I speak of lovers of poetry) who was not
alive in 1832 and old enough then to enjoy the
first perfect work of Tennyson, has had such a
sensation as that which was experienced in the
autumn of 1866 by readers of Mr. Swinburne's
" Poems and Ballads."   And I am sure that no
one in England has had any such sensation since.
The later revelation had indeed been preceded
by more signs and tokens than the earlier.
Tennyson's first work had passed unknown or
had been laughed at; at least two remarkable
volumes (not to mention " The Queen Mother "
and " Rosamond ") had already revealed to fit
readers what there was in Mr. Swinburne. The
chorus in " Atalanta," " Before the beginning of
years," had attracted the highest admiration
from impartial and unenthusiastic judges, while

it had simply swept younger admirers off their legs with rapture; and the lyrics of "Chastelard" had completed the effect in the way of exciting, if not of satisfying, expectation.

Now we were told, first, that a volume of extraordinarily original verse was coming out; now, that it was so shocking that its publisher repented its appearance; now, that it had been reissued, and was coming out after all. The autumn must have been advanced before it did come out, for I remember that I could not obtain a copy before I went up to Oxford in October, and had to avail myself of an expedition to town to "eat dinners" in order to get one. Three copies of the precious volume, with "Moxon" on cover and "John Camden Hotten" on title page, accompanied me back that night, together with divers maroons for the purpose of enlivening matters on the ensuing Fifth of November. The book was something of a maroon in itself as regards the fashion in which it startled people; and perhaps with youthful readers the hubbub did it no harm. We sat next afternoon, I remember, from luncheon time till the chapel bell rang, reading aloud by turns in a select company " Dolores " and " The Triumph of Time," " Laus Veneris " and " Faustine," and all the other wonders of the volume. There are some who say that after such a beginning critical appreciation is impossible,— the roses bloom too aggressively by the not at all calm Bendemeer when it is read again, and the pathetic and egotistic fallacies hide the truth from sight. If it were so, it were little use attempting to " correct impressions " in this or any similar matter. But I do not think so meanly of the human intellect. There is practically nothing for which it is impossible to " allow," nothing which may not be " ruled out." And though I feel that the maroons and the memories would make me a shamefully biassed judge of Mr. Swinburne personally, that I should if I were on a jury let him off on any accusation, and if I were a judge give him the smallest possible sentence the law allowed, a critical opinion of his works is a different matter. Everybody must keep a conscience and mind it somewhere; and, for

my part, I pride myself on keeping and mind-
ing it here.

Yet I have no hesitation in saying that after
these years I find myself disposed to alter very
little of the estimate which I made of the
" Poems and Ballads " as we read them " midst
triptychs and Madonnas," as another poet sings,
on that November Sunday. Mr. Swinburne
has done a very great deal of work since, and
I suppose not his wildest admirer would maintain that it has all or most of it been at the
level of the best parts of the " Poems and
Ballads." There are even, I believe, as there
usually are, archaics in Swinburnianism who
hold that it has never been really merry since
" Atalanta" itself; and, on the other hand,
there are more sober Swinburnians who perhaps question whether the poet's very best has
been seen except at intervals and in somewhat small proportion since the second " Poems
and Ballads" of 1878. Nor is it necessary to
spend much time in displaying the faults of
this most captivating of the poets of the second
half of the nineteenth century in England. The

danger of them, and to some extent the damage
of them, was seen in his very earliest work.
The astonishing fertility of his command of
language and of metre, the vast volume and
variety of his verbal music, were almost peril-
ously near to "carrying him away" then, and
no doubt have more and more actually done
so. I do not think that Mr. Swinburne has
ever written a single piece of verse that can be
called bad, or that does not possess qualities
of poetry which before his day would have
sufficed to give any man high poetical rank.
But he has always wanted discipline who never
wanted music or eloquence; and the complaint
that his readers sometimes find themselves
floating on and almost struggling with a cata-
ract of mere musical and verbal foam-water
is not without foundation. Of late years, too,
his extraordinary command of metre has led
him to make new and ever new experiments
in it which have been too often mere *tours de
force*, to plan sea-serpents in verse in order
to show how easily and gracefully he can make
them coil and uncoil their enormous length,

to build mastodons of metre that we may admire the proportion and articulation of their mighty limbs. In other words, he has sometimes, nay, too often, forgotten the end while exulting in his command of the means.

And yet, if we take the very latest of his works, how vast an addition to the possibilities of poetical delight do we see in it when compared with what English readers already had forty years ago, or even thirty! Although Mr. Swinburne's indebtedness to the late Laureate is of course immense, as must have been that of any man born when he was born, it happened most fortunately that his natural genius inclined him to the mode exactly opposite to Tennyson's. I have already endeavoured to show in these papers that, though that great poet could sing in divers tones, he always most inclined, and was most happily inspired when he did incline, to the mode of slow and languid singing. Mr. Swinburne's most natural gift is exactly the other way. His muse can "toll slowly" when she chooses; but she has always an impulse to

quicken, and is almost always happiest in quick
time.   Take, for instance, that famous poem already referred to, the great "Atalanta" chorus.
It is stately enough, and certainly not very
frolic in tone.   But what a race and rush there
is about it! What a thunder and charge of
verse! It is almost impossible even to read
it slowly. Take again the not less exquisite
song in "Chastelard," "Between the sundown
and the sea."   Here there is an appearance
of languor; there are no trisyllabic feet, none
of the extraneous aids to, or signs of, rhythmical speed.   And yet the measure hurries rather
than lags, the rhymes seem to invite each other
to respond and speed the response, the beginnings of the lines catch up and send on the
ends, the ends generate fresh beginnings almost
before they have ceased. So in the two magnificent pieces that come almost on the thresh-
old of the "Poems and Ballads" the same
irrepressible impulse may be observed. The
quatrain in which "Laus Veneris" is written
is one of the least lightly moving in appearance of all English measures, and yet it too

grows tumultuous; while the intricate and massive stanza of "The Triumph of Time" swells and swings like a wave.

In these cases the poet's idiosyncrasy is to some extent working against and subduing forms which do not lend themselves readily to it. But where the forms are congenial, the effect is too remarkable to have escaped even the most careless remark: and these pieces have in consequence supplied the most popular if not the most characteristic of Mr. Swinburne's poems. In that wonderful metre of "Dolores" and the Epilogue to the first "Poems and Ballads" which Mr. Swinburne adapted from Praed by shortening the last line, "the sound of loud water" and "the flight of the fires" both embody themselves in words. The mighty rush of the "Hymn to Proserpine," the galloping charge of the "Song in Time of Revolution," the dancing measures of "Rococo," and many others, attain what, speaking in jargon, one might call the maximum velocity of any British poet. It is sometimes, as, for instance, in "A Song in Time of Revo-

lution," very nearly impossible to make speech
accompany the words at the rate which seems
as if it were required. You gabble and stumble
in trying to keep up with the poet's speed.
And by degrees Mr. Swinburne developed and
perfected that faculty of his which has been
already noticed, — the faculty of arranging his
measures in a sort of antiphony, where, as in
very quick chanting, the alternate lines seem
to catch up their forerunners almost before
these have finished.

The two best examples of this curious gift
known to me, and two of the very best things
he has ever done, are the poems in the second
volume of " Poems and Ballads," entitled " At
a Month's End " and the " Dedication to Cap-
tain Richard Burton." I have sometimes had a
fancy that I should like to hear

> *"The night last night was strange and shaken,*
> *More strange the change of you and me,*
> *Once more for the old love's love forsaken*
> *We went down once more towards the sea,"*

with these unmatched passages which follow the
lines,

> " *As a star sees the sun and falters,*
>   *Touched to death by diviner eyes,*
>   *As on the old gods' untended altars*
>   *The old fire of withered worship dies,*"

sung by alternate semi-choruses, the second
tripping up the first a little. Nor is such a
motion as this,

> " *Nine years have risen and eight years set*
>   *Since there by the well-spring our hands on it met,*"

to be found anywhere in English poetry earlier.
The verse does not merely run, it *spins*, gyrat-
ing and revolving in itself as well as proceeding
on its orbit: the wave as it rushes on has
eddies and backwaters of live interior movement. All the metaphors and similes of water,
light, wind, fire, all the modes of motion, inspire
and animate this astonishing poetry.

VIII.

MR. SWINBURNE (*concluded*).

NOW if there is any truth in the view which was given in the last paper of Mr. Swinburne's poetical virtue, it will be seen at once that there is a special danger of uncritical admiration of him. The charm of the latest — let us hope not the last — of the Laureates is not an impetuous charm: it does not take you by a *coup de main;* but it never lets you go when it has once taken you. Has this other kind of poetical assault, this *ivresse de M. Swinburne,* (to borrow the phrase *ivresse de Victor Hugo* which was long ago used of the great French poet who was the God of Mr. Swinburne's idolatry,) the opposite defect of its opposite quality? Does it hold you with a grasp as insecure as the first onset of it is tempestuous? Is Mr. Swinburne a poetical Prince Rupert? There are some who say so. I seem to remember words of a very distinguished person, my own contemporary, about a man's "forgetting the *Poems and Ballads* he used to spout." All I can say is that I myself do not do anything of the kind. There are, as I take it, three kinds of literary lovers, as perhaps of other. There are those who only love one or a very few things and cleave to it or them. Perhaps this is the most excellent way, though I own I do not think so. There are the inconstants who love and who ride away. And there are those who are polygamous but faithful; that is to say, who constantly add to their loves, but never drop, forget, or slight the old. I boast myself to be of the last. In fact, why should a rational lover of poetry ever tire of Mr. Swinburne? That poet may have done things not wholly worthy of him, but no one is obliged to read them. He may have, even in his best things, been sometimes led astray by want of judgment in politics or religion or philosophy, by undue flux of language or of verse. But these things can be ignored or skipped. The virtue of the virtuous part re-

mains ; and I dare swear that it will be found at
the second reading and the tenth and the hundredth as distinct as at the first by those who
can get beyond and above mere novelty.

It is, if not the most philosophical, one of the
most effectual of tests to consider a very strong
literary mannerism or manner in its imitations. Mr. Swinburne, Heaven knows, has been
imitated enough. Kingsley says somewhere
that Amyas Leigh's companions proved the
presence of mosquitoes on the Magdalena "as
well as wretched men could." Reviewers did
the same with the influence of Mr. Swinburne.
For years his metres, his phrasing, his alliteration, his repetition of words, were the very
cophinus and *fœnum* of the poetaster, the sole
equipment and furniture with which he started
his dreadful trade. And did one poetaster or
poet during all these years achieve anything
with them that was not either designed or unconscious parody and that was worth anything?
Not one stanza, not one line. Some of the
designed parodies were very funny; some of
the undesigned ones funnier still. But that is a

proof of excellence, not of inferiority. It is
when a thing is imitable, not when it is paro-
diable, that it stands confessed as second-rate.
And Mr. Swinburne, like other poets on the
right side of the line, is not imitable, — at any
rate, he has not been imitated. They have
gotten his fiddle but not his rosin: they can
pile on alliteration, and be biblical in phrase,
and trench on things forbidden in subject, and
make a remarkably dull Italian into a god,
and a great but not rationally great Frenchman
into a compound of Shakespeare and Plato.
They can write lines in twenty-seven syllables
or thereabouts if necessary; but they can't write
poetry. Mr. Swinburne can and does.

There are, no doubt, several differences between poetical and other intoxication, but perhaps the chief difference is this. You can test
the strength of the liquids odious to Sir Wilfred
Lawson in two ways, — by dipping a Sykes's
hydrometer in them, or by actually imbibing and
waiting to see whether they " get you forrarder."
In the case of poetry, only the latter test is avail-
able : you are yourself the hydrometer. Conse-

quently it is exceedingly difficult to refer matters
to any common standard. "This is this to me
and that to thee." And it is nowhere so difficult
as in the case of a poet like Mr. Swinburne, whose
poetical appeal consists wholly or mainly in this
quality of impassioning and exhilarating. He
does not tell a story very well; his strictly dramatic faculty is not, I think, put by better judges
of drama than I am very high. He is not a
poetical schoolman and a poetical satirist like
Dryden, nor a poetical epigrammatist and con-
versationalist like Pope. What is more remarkable considering his century, he is not by any
means consummate or even eminent as a painter
in words. His sea-pieces put aside, it may be
said of his descriptions that, beautiful as they are,
they are rather decorative or conventional than
strictly pictorial, they do not bring the actual
sights before the eyes with the simple force of
Tennyson, or with the elaborate and complex
force of Rossetti and Mr. Morris. What he is
first of all is an absolutely consummate artist in
word-music of the current and tempestuous kind,
and an unfailing player on those moods of passion

or of thought which are akin to his own. And
if he fails in either of these two branches of his
appeal, I should say that it must be not so much
his fault as that of his audience. Music requires
an ear to hear as well as a voice to sing it; and
when Mr. Guppy remarked that "there are
chords in the human breast," his aposiopesis
might have been filled as well as in any other
way by the words "which, if their quality be not
of the right kind, will fail to respond to the very
deftest player." It may possibly be a fault of
Mr. Swinburne's that he lends himself rather ill
to mere dispassionate admiration. I doubt myself whether any poet of a very high class can
be dispassionately appreciated: but certainly he
cannot. You must, to quote one of his own
finest passages, be somewhat in the mood to

> "*Hear through star-proof trees*
> *The tempest of the Thyades*,"

or you must be in the mood of reaction after
such a hearing, in order to enjoy him fully.
"And what for no?" There is no *senatus con-
sultum de Bacchanalibus* as far as books are concerned; and I confess a certain contempt for

any one who cannot get excited over print and paper.

And after all there is a vast residuum when this merely personal excitement (which from my own experience I should say is quite as likely to be felt a little before fifty as a little after twenty) has subsided. There is the astonishing revelation of the metrical powers of English: for, though we knew them to be infinite before, this of itself does not take the very least thing off from the blush of each fresh instalment of the infinite surprises. There is the endless amusement of analysing the means (as to a certain limited effect is possible) by which these musical and emotional effects are produced. There is the pleasure of tracing what is, in so literary and scholarly a poet as Mr. Swinburne, the great and complicated indebtedness to the masters of Greece and of Rome, of Italy and of France, but most of all to those of England. And there is what is most delightful of all to the true lover of poetry and literature, the delight of finding out how much it is impossible to account for.

For to this we always come, and in this I
believe consists the greatest and most lasting
enjoyment of every kind of beauty. If you ever
could find out exactly why it is beautiful, the
thing would become scientific and cease to be
interesting. But you cannot, and so there is at
once the joy of possession and the ardour of the
unattained. You read for the first, the twentieth,
or the hundredth time "The Garden of Proserpine," or "Ilicet," or "A Wasted Vigil." There
is the first stage of pleasure, a purely uncritical
enjoyment. Then there is the second stage,
in which you sit down and take your critical
paper and pencil, and put down: metre so
much; alliteration so much; ingenious disposition of vowel sounds so much; criticism of life
so much; pathetic fancy so much; to having
read it when SHE was present, or absent, or
cross, or kind, or something, so much; literary
reminiscence so much. And then there is the
third, when you have totted these items up and
found that they do not come to anything like
the real total, that there is an infinite balance of
attraction and satisfaction which you cannot ex-

plain, which is fact, but an unsolved, unanalysed, ultimate fact. The poetry which has come to mean this to a lover of poetry never gets stale, never loses charm, never seems the same, or rather, always being the same in one way, is always fresh in another.

Among such poetry I, for my part, rank a very large proportion of Mr. Swinburne's earlier work, and not a very little of his later. If it were ever going to pall on me, I think it pretty certainly must have palled by this time. And what is more, there is the comforting reflection that anything in which one has taken delight so long is secure from palling by the very fact. The accumulation of delighted remembrance is a delight in itself: what has been has been, and therefore must ever continue to be. The constantly repeated thought and sensation has become an entity, a thing in itself, a possession for ever, by the very dint of having been so long and so often possessed.

IX.

MACAULAY.

THERE are not many deities who find a place in every Pantheon or are represented by attributes in every system of monotheism. But of these is Nemesis; and of Nemesis I do not hesitate to proclaim myself a devout and fearful worshipper. The great name which stands at the head of this paper is perhaps in literary history something of an example of her power. Such a hero-of-Dr.-Smiles, such a *Selfelpista* (as the Italians I believe call it), has never been known since the lucky literary men of the Age of Anne, whom he himself described in some of his boldest and most effective strokes. Macaulay, though not low-born, was born quite in the middle class; he inherited nothing worth speaking of; and he did not devote himself to any of the ordinary paying professions. Whether —a circumstance over which his biographers

skim rather lightly — he did definitely rat at
an early period of life from Toryism to Liberalism does not very much matter. He was born
a Liberal of the type which he was to do so
much to multiply and foster; and if his hoisting
of that flag was a little prompted by considera-
tions of probable profit, we may very well set
the thing off against a very similar incident in
the career of Canning in the generation before,
and agree to say nothing about it.

From almost his earliest manhood Macaulay's
life was a sort of cascade of fallings on his feet.
He came just at the period when clear, brilliant,
confident, and rather shallow review-writing was
at its best paid and most honoured apogee. He
came at the time when there were still rotten
boroughs to bring forward a young man of
talent, and when a young man of talent could
make his position sure by denouncing the
rotten boroughs on which he had risen. In
the Reform Bill debates there was no young
man of anything like his talent on the other
side, and the one young or youngish man who
would have been too much for him in posi-

tion and natural eloquence, as well as a fair
match for him in scholarship and knowledge,
Stanley, was by historical accident on the same
side. In society he coincided with the period
of breakfasts, and belonged to a party in which
there was nobody to match him as talker
except Sydney Smith, who was getting old.
When it was necessary to provide for himself solidly, the least troublesome and most
paying of all appointments left for any one to
obtain came in his way. He stayed in India
long enough to pick up a competence and not
long enough to damage his health. He had no
tastes, either domestic or luxurious, which could
interfere with this independence, or impose on
him a longer servitude. He came home and settled down to his own ideal life: a little politics,
a great deal of historical literature, and as much
society as he chose, without any obligations of
family estate or office to force more on him.
His great history fell on the very nick of time
to suit its merits, and the famous twenty thousand pound cheque symbolised at once those
merits and their reward. And then too he had

6

the crowning felicity of an opportune death.
Had Macaulay lived to the age of Lord Sherbrooke, something like Lord Sherbrooke's fate
might — indeed I think must — have been his,
though the few years' difference between them
must have given him a slight advantage. It is
almost terrible to think of the feelings of the
man who prophetically described Mr. Gladstone
half a century ago, when he found himself face
to face with the choice of ceasing to be a Liberal
or becoming a Gladstonian.

Yet Nemesis has been even with him (as she
always is) for all these good things, and for the
enormous popularity which was partly their
result and partly their complement. Almost
immediately after his death began a steady dead
set of critical depreciation, which, unhasting,
unresting, has attacked him ever since and which
for some years past has spread from the critics
to the vulgar. The decriers of Macaulay have
been a strangely miscellaneous band. It was
not to be expected that the Tories whom he
affected to despise should like him; or that the
Evangelicals, who regarded him as a renegade,

and the Dissenters, who looked on him as the
inheritor of the wicked wit of Sydney Smith,
should love him. But he managed to attract
hosts of enemies of the most heterogeneous
kinds. It used to be a tradition in Oxford (I
never saw the passage and I apologise to Mr.
Smith if it is not true) that Mr. Goldwin Smith
even in the fullest days of his Liberalism called
Macaulay "a shallow scoundrel." Mr. Matthew
Arnold, as is well known, exhausted his elegant
quiver on the "Lays of Ancient Rome," and was
evidently often thinking of Macaulay when he
denounced the British Philistine. The tribe of
Dryasdust hated him because he was not merely
an omnivorous reader but a brilliant writer; and
the devotees of historical philosophy could not
forgive him his obstinate superficiality and the
calm assumption which accompanied it that there
was nothing beneath the surface. Although one
considerable Mediævalist, Mr. Freeman, used to
take his part, for reasons not very difficult of
discovery, it was impossible for any other student of the older ages not to resent the bland
ignoring of something like a thousand years of

English history which made Macaulay constantly
infer, and sometimes almost say, that nobody
need look beyond the Great Rebellion.

Also I am afraid it must be said, though it will
make one devoted Macaulayan who is a great
friend of mine wroth, that the number of Macaulay's enemies in a certain sense is sure to in-
crease by just so many people as undertake a
serious study of any person or period with whom
or which he has dealt. It is the general if not
the universal result in such cases that the inquir-
ers declare that Macaulay, if not thoroughly dishonest, is at least thoroughly untrustworthy. It
is not that he is a partisan, — history without
partisanship is to my fancy, in the old phrase of
King Henry the Fifth, like "beef without mus-
tard." Nor is it that he is, in history, deliber-
ately unfair. In his anonymous work, where a
man ought to be most careful, I fear he sometimes was. Some of the imputations on Croker
in the "Boswell" Essay are utterly inexcusable,
even if we did not know, as we do, that the
reviewer took up the book he intended to review
with a determination to "slate" it. But having

had occasion to examine more than one part of
the " History " carefully and documents in hand,
I do not think that this sort of unfairness is often
to be found there. Unfortunately, another sort
which is common in the " Essays" is common
also in the " History." I do not hold that Macaulay, unless (as in the Warren Hastings case)
he was himself misled by his authorities, ever
advances against his " black beasts" anything
which is positively untrue. I do not urge that
he often suppresses, in a way with which much
fault can be found, anything which makes in
their favour. But he has a less gross, perhaps,
but a worse and more dangerous fault than any
of these. He is constantly misleading by in-
nuendo suggestive of the false, by epithets, by
generalisations, by rhetorical extensions of the
actual fact or text. He finds in his document,
let us say, that A. on not certain authority was
accused on a particular occasion of doing or
saying such and such a thing. This trans-
lates itself in the pages of the History into
a general charge against A. of being notoriously in the habit of saying or doing it. A

particular phrase is reported of a particular person: Macaulay always turns it to "men began to say," or something of that kind. In short, the most careful student, the most experienced critic, never quite knows where to have this great historian on a subject which he, the student or critic, has not yet examined for himself; and when he does examine for himself he too often has to ask himself, Is it possible that these colourings and baits to the unwary, these suppressions by dint of shading, and suggestions by careless scattering of adjectives and adverbs, can have been made without a deliberate *parti pris*, without the aim of the advocate whose admitted and professional privilege it is to throw dust in the eyes of the jury if he possibly can?

Something else has to be added. They have made Macaulay into school-books, and it is well known that, if it be possible to instil disgust and horror of an author into all but the few whom the not perhaps quite equal Jove of literature has specially loved, it can be done most easily and completely by setting them to learn him at school.

And so my Lord Macaulay of late — though
I do not know that the great heart of the people
has yet been affected about him, or that that
Australian book-shelf of which we have all heard
has yet been denuded of the " Essays " — has
begun to fall rather on evil days. The set
against him has spread from the highest to the
lowest rank of critics; the lady novelist has
lifted up what it may be almost improper to
call her heel against him; you see superior
gibes to his address in those curious periodicals
of scraps and patches which appear more than
anything else to satisfy the literary hunger and
thirst of the end of the nineteenth century. It
is whispered, apropos of the miserable Mont-
gomery, and in connection with the present in-
fluentially supported movement for roasting all
reviewers gratis, that Macaulay was one of the
wicked critics who delight to "slate" good
authors. Fond as we are nowadays of rehabili-
tations, the rehabilitator has not come to him.
In short, Nemesis is upon him: the deferred
discount of that twenty thousand pound cheque
has to be paid, and it is heavy.

X.

MACAULAY (*concluded*).

I DO not know that there have been any very
striking vicissitudes in my own opinions of
Macaulay. I used to delight in the "Essays"
when I was a young boy, and I do not delight
in them much less now that I am neither a boy
nor young. But I think I always had a kind of
inkling of the defects, which has gained in pre-
cision and definiteness, but has not, I think,
deepened much. I still think that, on any subject which Macaulay has touched, his survey is
unsurpassable for giving a first bird's-eye view,
and for creating interest in the matter. Of course
for those readers who have what is called "the
faith of the charcoal-burner," who must be per-
mitted to repose absolute implicit reliance on
every detail of the narrative, every clause of the
creed set before them, or who else will be mis-

erable, Macaulay is the most dangerous of all possible guides. But it must be an exceedingly moderate intelligence which does not pretty quickly perceive the classes and kinds of subject on which he is to be taken with grains of salt, an exceedingly sluggish and clumsy intellect which cannot apply these grains with sufficient discretion.

And he certainly has not his equal anywhere for covering his subject in the pointing-stick fashion. You need not — you had much better not — pin your faith on his details, but his Pisgah sights are admirable. Hole after hole — a very sieveful of holes indeed — has been picked in the "Clive" and the "Hastings," the "Johnson" and the "Addison," the "Frederick" and the "Horace Walpole." Yet every one of these papers contains sketches, summaries, *précis*, which have not been made obsolete or valueless by all the work of correction in detail. As a literary critic, again, Macaulay is far from impeccable. His sympathies were not very wide, and they were apt to be conditioned by attractions and repulsions quite other than

literary. Although he had had a strictly classical education, although he early showed remarkable mastery of literary form himself, it cannot
be said that this form was ever the object of any
but a very subordinate share of his attention.
It is amazing, when one has long been familiar
with his essay — an extremely interesting one —
on Temple, and then comes to be familiar with
Temple's own work, to find how little Macaulay
seems to have relished or realised Temple's
purely literary excellence. He was a good
Italian scholar and something of a Dantist; yet
his remarks on the second of the three great
poets of the world are wofully narrow and in-
adequate. I feel morally certain that he could
not have been the Miltonian that he was if
Milton had been a Cavalier and a Churchman;
and I doubt whether it was not necessary for
him to make up his mind (as he did on next to
no evidence) that Bunyan served in the Parlia-
mentary army before he could give a voice to
his admiration of "The Pilgrim's Progress."
Even when politics did not interfere, it is obvious that his interest in literature as a round of

sketches of ethics, of manners, of political life in
the wide sense, altogether overtops his interest
in it as literature. On Spenser, he has, as
everybody knows, fallen into one of his rare
blunders of fact. He had read, as he had read
everything, the minor Elizabethans; but they
excite no rapture in him. It is admitted that
he has made Bacon, no very deep metaphysi-
cian at best, shallower and more exoteric still
in his exposition of him. It is " man in relation
to the Town " that he, like his beloved Addison,
really cares for.

Enough was said in the former paper on this
subject of the defects of Macaulay as a historian; and indeed they are not deniable by
any competent judge who is not for the nonce
a mere advocate. But the merit which has been
allowed to his Essays, that of extraordinarily
vivid presentation of the subject, must be allowed
here to a still greater degree, inasmuch as it is
shown on a far greater scale and in much more
difficult matter. With part of the period which
Macaulay's History covers I happen, as has been
said, to have acquainted myself in considerable

detail and by going to the original authorities. Nobody can possibly be more opposed to Macaulay's general views on the politics of that period than I am. And yet I am disposed to think and say, without the least conscious intention of paradox and with much deliberate guarding against it, that of no other period of English history does an idea so clear, vivid, and on the whole accurate exist in so large a number of people, and that this is due to Macaulay. The fact is that the power of making historical periods and transactions real and living is an exceedingly rare power, and that Macaulay had it. Since his day we have had a numerously attended school of historians who have gone beyond even Macaulay in book-devouring, who have as a rule confined themselves more than he did to single periods, and who have sometimes exhausted their powers of picturesque writing and their readers' patience in severely accurate detail. Not one of them, to my thinking, has achieved the success of making his period living and actual as Macaulay has. The picturesque people hide the truth with their

flashes and their flourishes. The Dryasdusts
dole it out in such cut and dried morsels,
with such a lack of art, such a tedious tyranny
of document and detail, that the wood almost literally becomes invisible because of the
trees.

As for the "Lays of Ancient Rome," and the
not very numerous but very remarkable minor
verse which completes them, the history of that
division of Macaulay's works is the most start-
ling and the best known of all. When the
"Lays" first appeared, they took the world by
storm, and they held it for many years pretty
well unquestioned. Nobody in his senses, of
course, ever took them for the highest poetry:
they cannot in that respect pretend to vie even
with their own author's curious fragment on
"The Last Buccaneer," or his exquisite "Jaco-
bite's Epitaph." But in one of the kinds of
poetry just below the very highest they exhibited accomplishment and mastery quite wonderful, and gave the poetical satisfaction to
thousands, and probably millions, who were not
fitted to receive it from higher things. Then

arose Mr. Matthew Arnold and denounced them
as "pinchbeck," and the large number of persons who about five and twenty years ago were
convinced that to get "culture" you must go
to Mr. Arnold, at once echoed "pinchbeck,"
and vowed that they had never thought them
anything else. Those, however, who had not
exactly waited for Mr. Arnold to form their
opinions of classical and romantic perfection,
were not, I think, much disturbed by this contempt. And in fact "pinchbeck" is about the
unluckiest epithet that Mr. Arnold could have
selected. Pinchbeck in the literal sense pretends to be gold, and pinchbeck in the trans-
ferred sense means anything which pretends
to be something it is not. Now the "Lays"
pretend to be nothing that they are not; they
aim at nothing more than a rattling spirited
presentation in easy ballad rhyme of pictu-
resquely told incidents. There is no doubt
plenty of pinchbeck in English verse. There
is the pinchbeck that imitates Greek tragedy
and the pinchbeck that imitates mediæval imagery; there is pinchbeck which would fain be

French and pinchbeck which would fain be philosophical. I am not quite certain that some of
Mr. Arnold's own verse, exquisite as is the best
of it, is not pinchbeck in its affectation of a sort
of pseudo-philosophic attitude dashed with scep-
tical modernism, and corrected by classic form.
But there is no pinchbeck in the " Lays," because there is no pretence. Gold perhaps they
are not; silver I think they are; copper an unkind or partial judgment may call them. But
not twenty Mr. Arnolds shall ever persuade me
that they are base metal, — metal which shams
a higher stuff.

I think the publication of Sir George Trevel-
yan's excellent life of his uncle began a reaction
in favour of Macaulay, and I think that reaction,
though not very sudden or violent, is solidly
founded and will go on. The pedants indeed
are, I hear, raging at him more than ever; but
they can do little harm; and the average half-
educated journalist has begun to leave off thinking it fine to sneer at him. He will never of
course regain the position that he held during
the last decade of his own life and for a few

years afterwards: and I should be sorry if he did. For his thought was no doubt distinctly *borné* and sometimes almost vulgar; his style was sometimes flashy and almost always deficient in the finest distinction; he was a terribly partial historian; and in every department of literature he was insensible to, and incapable of recognising, *nuances*, half-tones, delicate contrasts, subtle gradations. But on the other hand he had that rarest and most precious power of attracting his readers to, and interesting them in, subjects that were not merely frivolous or ephemeral; his mental attitude was sturdy, honest, shrewd; he had a stout and noble patriotism; his very partisanship, his very advocacy, had something manly and downright in its unfeigned and unmistakable character; and fatiguing as his "snip-snap" sometimes is, utterly disgusting as are imitations of it, yet any one who speaks of Macaulay's style with contempt seems to me to proclaim himself fatally and finally as a mere " one-eyed man " in literary appreciation. Of the merits and defects of that curious generation of middle-class Liberalism which flourished in England from 1830 to 1860, he is probably the most striking example; and even if he were not this, he is a very great man of letters, and an almost unsurpassed leader to reading.

XI.

BROWNING.

WHENEVER it happens to me to write about Robert Browning, I am always a little apprehensive of the fate of the Trimmer. I have loved and admired his work for full thirty years; but I do not belong to any of the four parties wherein most of mankind are included as regards him. There are those who were Browningites from the first, or almost the first, and have been faithful all through, — a race now naturally diminishing by efflux of time. There are those who began to like him after he himself began to be fashionable, and who, whether they have gone the whole way with the Browning Society or not, regard him as one of the greatest of poets and philosophers. There are those who, from the sturdy English stand-point, have always been unable to tolerate him at all, at whatever time he was presented to

them. And there are those who, though chrono-
logically contemporaries of the rage for him,
either had other rages which kept them from
appreciating him, or are young enough (not
necessarily in years) to think him already *vieux
jeu.* All these are more or less "prevailing
parties," as Lord Foppington says, and can
encourage one another by dint of fellowship.

But my case is a little different. It so happened that Browning never fell in my way when
I was a boy, except in very small and casual
extracts. These I owed, I think, chiefly to that
godsend to the youth of the late fifties and early
sixties, Dr. Holden's "Foliorum Silvula," which,
if it was the occasion of much deplorable Greek
and Latin verse, must have laid the foundation
of acquaintance with the very best of English.
I cannot remember reading a single volume of
Browning as a volume before I became an undergraduate. But the collected edition of his
Poems appeared almost directly afterwards, and
I got it, while no long time passed before the
appearance of "Dramatis Personæ." Then I
became very much addicted to Browning, and

used to read him night and day. I have never myself quite understood what people meant and still sometimes seem to mean by the "obscurity," the "difficulty" of "Sordello." It is distinctly breathless and it is unduly affected; but if anybody has got a brain at all, that brain ought not to be very much exercised in following the fortunes of Sordello and Taurello, Alberic and Ezzelin, Adelaide and the rest. It appeared to me that "Paracelsus" did n't prove much, and like "Sordello" was breathless, while I did not and do not care much more for Aprile than for Paul Dombey. But who could miss the splendid, and for its date, wholly novel poetry of it? The plays were mainly a bore — I have scarcely ever read a serious play younger than the seventeenth century that was not more or less of a bore to me — but there too the poet appeared. And as for "Men and Women," and the "Lyrics," and so forth, there was no possible mistake about them, when they were at their best. I never loved the most popular pieces much. "Ghent to Aix" is only a *tour de force*, and I can remember that when as a boy I first

heard of it I thought that the good man rode to
Aix in Provence (which would have been something like a ride), and was desperately disappointed at the actual achievement. In "Count
Gismond" there is a passage of four and a half
lines which is good enough for anything, but the
rest is no great matter. "The Glove" contains
other lines which stick in the memory, but the
moral is mainly rubbish, and Marot *was* a poet.

And so on and so on. But I had never read,
and I have never read, anything like even the
least of half a hundred of the others in its best
parts. "Christina" (what devil ever tempted
Mr. Browning to run the double lines of the
earlier version into single ones?); "In a Gondola" and "The Last Ride together," which I
will uphold for two of the best love poems of
the century, be the others what they may, the
last named being perhaps the very best that we
have produced for two hundred years; "Mes-
merism" and "Porphyria's Lover," a pair on
a plane only a little lower; the first stanza of
"Meeting at Night," in which Browning has for
once met and matched his great contemporary

and rival on his own ground; the delightful
rococo of "Women and Roses"; yet another
pair, "Life in a Love" and "Love in a Life";
"Love among the Ruins" and "Two in the Cam-
pagna," which ought, like so many of Browning's poems, to be taken together; "Prospice,"
great among the greatest, and such a quiet
essence of heroic combativeness that I never
could understand how my friend Mr. Henley
failed to include it in his "Lyra Heroica";
"Childe Roland," best of its own class, though
"The Flight of the Duchess" runs it hard;
and crowning the whole "Rabbi ben Ezra"; —
these were things (and I have not mentioned a
quarter of my own favourites) to set the blood
coursing rarely.   And yet, though I believe I
love and loved them with a sum that twenty
thousand members of Browning Societies could
not make up, I never could and cannot now
call myself exactly a Browningite.   Even then,
even in his heyday, the man (it is surely per-
missible to use slang of one who used so
much) "jawed" at times; he was not to be
depended upon for certainty of taste or touch;

he would drop hideous negligences or more hideous outrages of intention in the middle of a masterpiece; it was clear that he wanted to teach; and so forth.

The works which followed "Dramatis Personæ" were not very well suited to convert a half-hearted though at times intense worshipper of this kind into a whole-hearted one. I am told that "The Ring and the Book" did actually bring about that change which its author anticipated in the famous address to the British public who "might like him yet." I cannot say that it brought about a contrary change in me. A man does not once appreciate to the full "The Last Ride together," or "Love among the Ruins," and get tired of them afterwards. But I own that this huge poem itself gave me little pleasure. Of course there are fine things in it, and the traits of "criticism of life" as well as the achievements of poetical expression are often admirable. But it is so tyrannously long without any action; so mercilessly voluble without much justification for the volubility; it has such a false air of wisdom and philosophy

which is after all not particularly recondite or
novel, — that I remember thinking of "Porphyria's Lover," and wishing that some one had
applied that person's drastic procedure to the
poet on his own principles.

Nevertheless I persevered, much enduring,
and except "Red Cotton Nightcap Country,"
which I do not believe I have ever read through
yet, and "People of Importance," which I
missed by accident and have never picked up,
I do not believe there is a volume or a line of
Browning's that I have not read. It was tribu-
lation mostly in those days, but there was
comfort sometimes. "Fifine" is really a great
book (the Browningites, I am told, do not like
it), and there are gleanings even in the volumes
where Mr. Browning thought to make up for a
not wholly perfect knowledge of Greek by call-
ing a Nymph a "numph." And at the evening
time there was light. Even in the darkest days
of the *Conciones ad Vulgus Browningense* appeared flashes of the old splendour, never seen
on any other land or sea; the final poem of
"Pachiarotto" was an almost flawless gem, and

the latest volumes of all, especially "Asolando," showed a wonderful recovery. It was a case of *eripitur persona, manet res.* The mask that the Browning Society had admired, and that had been constantly touched up and made more mask-like to please it, fell off, and Browning — not in his first vigour, not as when he wrote "In a Gondola" or "After," but still Browning — reappeared.

It is of course a very great misfortune to be thus constitutionally unable to be "in the tune." In 1863 one ran the risk of being thought an affected and presumptuous youth for saying that, whatever faults "Sordello" might have, it was not half so obscure as even then one of Mr. Gladstone's speeches was; and that "The Last Ride together" was worth the weight of the lady and her lover and their horses in gold. In 1883 one ran the risk of being dismissed as a griz- zling fossil because one failed to admire volume after volume of blank-verse "jaw," where for the most part mannerism took the place of thought and facile ruggedness that of originality. I am not sure that in 1894 the light, light wheel is not already on the point of turning again, and that anybody who admires Browning at all will not be soon despised as something or other — it really does not much matter what. Nevertheless, as there are nearly always the seven thousand or thereabouts who have not bowed the knee to the Baal of any particular moment, who do not take their admirations or their dislikes at the stall which happens to be prescribed by fashion, it may not be impertinent to examine a little further the reasons which have made one person of the class a lover of Browning who was never a Browningite, — a critic of Browning, who never would join in the cry about " harshness " and " obscurity," and all the rest of it. If outsiders do indeed see most of the game, such a one should at any rate have been able to see a little of it ; and perhaps even his enthusiasm may cease to be suspected when it is taken in conjunction with his objections.

XII.

BROWNING (*concluded*).

I DO not know that there is any English writer to whom the motto *Qualis ab incepto* may be applied with more propriety than to Robert Browning, — any whose works are more intimately connected with his life. I am not one of those who take a very great interest in the biography of poets, and I think that its importance as illustrating their works has been as a rule exaggerated. But certainly, if a tolerably instructed student of books and men were set the problem of Browning's works without any knowledge of Browning's life, it would not give him much trouble to lay down the main lines of the latter. A man who had had to write for a living, or to devote himself to writing in the intervals of any regular occupation, could hardly have produced so much and have produced it with such a complete disregard of

the public taste and the consequent chances of
profit. A man who had had the advantages
of that school and university education which
as a rule happens to the upper and upper-
middle classes of Englishmen would hardly
have produced his work with such an entire
disregard of authority as well as of popularity.
The first influence was no doubt wholly good,
for, copy-books notwithstanding, the instances
of men who without private means or practical
sinecures have produced large quantities of
very fine poetry are very rare, and for the last
couple of centuries almost non-existent. The
circumstances of Browning's education, on the
other hand, no doubt had a good influence as
well as a bad. It is open to any one to contend
that his natural genius was too irregular, too
recalcitrant to the file, to have admitted the
labour of that instrument; and that therefore,
if he had had a classical and critical taste im-
planted in him, the struggle of the two would
have condemned him to silence. But it is quite
certain that his worst faults are exactly those
of a privately educated middle-class English-

man, and it is of the very highest interest to
compare his career and performance in this
respect with the career and performance of
Mr. Ruskin, who was in many respects his
analogue in genius and circumstances, but
whose sojourn at Oxford gave just the differ-
entiating touch.

Allow however, as we may, less or more influence to these things, I think it will hardly
be denied that the effect manifested itself very
early, and that even by the appearance of
" Bells and Pomegranates " prediction of their
author's characteristics and career as a whole
was pretty easy. It certainly had become so
by the time that I myself, as I have said,
was " entered " in Browning. It was obvious
on the credit side that here was a man with
an almost entirely novel conception of poetical vocabulary and style, with a true and wonderful lyrical gift, with a faculty of argument
and narrative in verse which, diametrically as
it was opposed in kind to the Drydenian tradition, had been in kind and volume unsurpassed since Dryden, and with an enormous

range and versatility of subject. He could, it was clear, not merely manipulate words and verse in a manner almost suggesting prestidigitation, but was also much more than a mere word- and metre-monger. On certain sides of the great problem of life he could think with boldness and originality, if not with depth: the depth of Mr. Browning's thought belongs to the same mistaken tradition as his obscurity, and reminds me of those inky pools in the limestone districts which look and are popularly reputed to be bottomless till somebody tries them and finds them to be about nineteen foot two. He had above all a command of the most universally appealing, if not also the loftiest, style of poetry, — that which deals with love, — hardly equalled except by the very greatest, and not often excelled even by them.

But these great merits were accompanied by uncommon and sometimes very ugly defects. It was obvious that his occasional cacophonies and vulgarities were not merely an exaggeration of his recognition of the truth that the vernacular can be made to impart

vigour, and that discords and degradations
of scale and tone heighten and brighten musical effects. They were at any rate sometimes
clearly the result of a combination of indolence and bad taste, — indolence that would not
take the trouble to remove, bad taste that did
not fully perceive the gravity of the blemishes
that wanted removing in his very finest passages. There was also that most fatal defect
which the ill-natured fairy so often annexes
to the gifts of vigorous and fertile command
of language, — an excessive voluminousness
and volubility. Lastly there was the celebrated
" obscurity," which taken to pieces and judged
coolly was simply the combined result of the
good and bad gifts just mentioned. Mr. Browning had plenty to say on whatsoever subject he
took up; he had a fresh, original, vigorous
manner of saying it; he was naturally inclined
to and had indulged his inclination for odd
and striking locutions; he was very allusive;
and he was both impatient of the labour of
correction and rather insensitive to the necessity of it. Hence what he himself has rather

damagingly called in a probably unintentional
satire and caricature of himself the " monstr'
inform' ingens-horrendous demoniaco-seraphic
penman's latest piece of graphic " which occurs
so often in his work, which the admirers take
for something very obscure but very precious,
requiring the aid of Browning dictionaries and
so forth, which the honest public gapes at,
from which the primmer kind of academic
critic turns away disgusted, and which more
catholic and tolerant appreciation regards, if
not exactly with disgust, certainly with regret
and disapproval.

Now it was practically certain that when, from
such a man, the very last restraining or dissuad-
ing checks in the shape of public disapproval or
(more powerful still) indifference were removed,
he would take the bit in his teeth and run away
with himself. This was what Browning practically did in the score of volumes in improvised
blank verse chiefly, but also in other metres,
which he poured forth after 1868. The greater
part of this matter I feel tolerably confident
that futurity will relegate to the same shelf

with Southey's epics and Dryden's plays. Indeed, I myself would much rather read the worst of either group than " Prince Hohenstiel Schwangau," or the "Balaustion" books. But if the said posterity is well served by its editors, from time to time certain things will be rescued from even this part, and, added to the earlier harvest, will form a poetical *corpus* not by any means contemptible in respect of bulk even when ranked with the sheaves of pretty fertile poets, and full of admirable if rarely perfect poetry. Few philosophical poets have lived long — Lucretius and Dante are the only great exceptions — and I am as certain as it is not rash to be that Mr. Browning in his philosophical pieces will not rank with these. Indeed, it was not much of a philosophy, this which the poet half echoed from and half taught to the second half of the nineteenth century. A sort of undogmatic Theism heightened by a very little undogmatic Christianity; a theory of doing and living more optimist than Carlylism and less fantastic than Ruskinism, but as vague and as unpractical as either;

8

a fancy for what is called analogy and a marvellous gift of rhetorical exposition, — these
made it up. It looks vast enough and various
enough in form and colour at a distance; it
shrinks and crumbles up pretty small when
you come to examine it.

But a poet is always saved by his poetry,
and of that, thank Heaven, Mr. Browning had
plenty to secure his salvation. Those volumes
of selections by which in an even narrower
compass than that already hinted at he is perhaps destined to live most securely and long-
est (though the second wants refreshing and
rearranging) display a perfect Aurora Borealis
of poetical flashes of the intensest luminosity
and the most endless variety of colour. The
sabre-and-stirrup clang of the *i* rhymes in
" Through the Metidja "; the astonishingly
various music and imagery of the songs of " In
a Gondola "; the steady hopeless swing — too
full of passion for rant — of " The Last Ride ";
the strange throbbing measure of " Mesmer-
ism "; and a hundred other things which I
must not mention lest after the string given

in the last paper I be accused of mere cata-
logue-making; — these are the things which
generation after generation of lovers of poetry
will read and rejoice in, just as we now read
and rejoice in Donne and Marvell, and the
rest of the seventeenth century lyrists. Indeed, I sometimes wonder whether on one of
their sides Browning did not come nearer to
these than Coleridge or Shelley, Keats or Tennyson. For if he had not the finest seventeenth century magic in remoteness of matter
and melody of form, he had the odd ups and
downs, the queer admixture of ore and dross,
the want of criticism, the incompleteness which
mark all but one or two of our seventeenth
century men.

And if any one must needs, to complete his
idea of a great poet, have something more than
poetry and passion, than music and moonlight,
I shall at least allow that Browning's life philosophy, if exposed to the criticisms made above,
did once or twice, notably in the above-mentioned
" Rabbi ben Ezra," receive a very noble and
lasting enshrinement and expression. A little

optimist perhaps, but certainly not with the
optimism which blinks the facts of life; a little
pantheistic, as perhaps are all the great religions
and all the great philosophies when you come
to examine them from certain points of view and
mood; a trifle unsubstantial, as divine philosophy must always be. But full of a generous
and indomitable spirit, free from the whining
and cavilling to which poetic philosophy so
often inclines ; throbbing with that remembrance of delight which is perhaps better than
any delight itself; not covetous but not despair-
ing of more; content to comprehend as far as
may be, to labour as much as need be, to hope
as much as is rational, — the philosophy in short
of a poet who is also a man, which duplicate
advantage poets have not always possessed.

XIII.

DICKENS.

THERE are few comparatively recent writers about whom it is more difficult to write at the present moment than it is to write about Dickens. Current public opinion about him seems to have got into a kind of tangle, and there are as many as four or five distinct views regarding him, all of which are held by considerable parties, each including some who deserve consideration quite independent of the numbers of their companions. There are — perhaps least numerous at the moment, but including, I fancy, a larger genuine number of genuine adherents than some of the other parties would admit — the old thorough Dickens worshippers, who more or less represent the public that Dickens himself took by storm. These have a relish for his fun, and are not too critical over his pathos; they are not revolted by, or at least can pardon, and sometimes they

directly sympathise with, his eccentric and ill-
reasoned politics and sociology; they do not
care to inquire too curiously into his formal peculiarities of plot and management; they do not
cavil at, perhaps they enjoy, his style. Some
of them indeed, who have literary gifts, follow
him more or less directly to this day. Then, to
take as nearly as I can their chronological suc-
cessors, there are those who, admitting that he
was a genius, feeling a genuine enjoyment of his
humour, and allowing him a great amount of
credit for marvellous inventive power, dwell
strongly on all the excepted points just hinted
at, and in addition resent not merely the extraordinary topsy-turvyness and the sharp limits of
his power of delineation of character, but also
that quality in him which can only be called
vulgarity, though I admit all the objections
which are often urged against the use of that
word as itself vulgar. This class is not by any
means a homogeneous one, and the degrees in
which its members allow the positive or credit
side to overcome the negative or debit in their
general estimate are extremely various.

But independent of these two parties, at least three more, among men mostly, but not always, younger than the members of the other two, admit of definition more or less exact. There are those who are simply "tired of Dickens," who resent the frequency with which his characters have passed into the range of newspaper quotation and parallel, who would like to "turn the page," who are in fact bored by him. There is a still larger body among the very young who think him out of date in more than time, and who wonder how anybody can even think of Dickens when he might read Mr. Hardy and Mr. Meredith. And there is a small body again, very heterogeneously composed, but including some persons of wit if also of crotchet, who would if they could exalt Dickens as a great democratic genius, as one who made his way without and in spite of education, fashion, powerful connections, and so forth, and vindicated the rights of the faculties of genius pure and simple.

There is something of an egg- or sword-dance in the attempt at a criticism of Dickens amid these delicate and dangerous differences of opinion. But perhaps we shall find that adherence to the personal and historical side of the matter here, as elsewhere, will help us not a little. It has, I believe, been held by the fanciful, that a man of tolerably healthy mind, who does not allow himself to be hampered by prejudice or crotchet, usually goes through a kind of microcosm of all possible opinions about his subject; and though this may be something of an exaggeration, it is also something of a truth.

I began myself very young (at ten or twelve years old, I should think) with "Pickwick," and I own that I should not to this day think much of any one who began at about that age with "Pickwick" and did not adore it. I will add, that I should not think very much of anyone who materially altered his opinion of "Pickwick," however many years he might live and however many times he might read it afterwards. Years will indeed bring the philosophic mind to this extent, that one perceives more and more the extremely artificial character of the Pickwickian world. But then a boy does not take the Pickwickian world for a natural one. He simply

does not think of it either as natural or unnatural; and when the sense of its artificiality
comes on him, it destroys nothing, it brings
about no disillusion, it only adds a certain con-
dition to his view. I do not think that to this
day I ever allow more than a year or two to
pass without reading "Pickwick" through from
beginning to end; and I cannot perceive any
marked diminution in the satisfaction with which
I do so. As Mr. Boswell, in one of his inimit-
able compromises between the simpleton and
the sage, somewhere remarks, "I seldom experience less disappointment in any scheme of
happiness I trace out." And this, I think, is
the very hardest test to which anything, literary
or other, can be put. It is all very well to say
that youthful enjoyment induces a strong delu-
sion, and that we rather refuse to acknowledge
a diminution than actually experience an equal-
ity. If this be so, why do other things in which
I used to take quite as much delight as in " Pickwick " fail to give me the same pleasure now?
No; I shall maintain that this impossible and
burlesque epopee of the four friends has a

quality in it which belongs only to the literature which is pre-eminently good in a kind just short of the highest.

But, it will be said, " Pickwick " is not all Dickens, and all Dickens is not " Pickwick," both of which propositions are most undeniably true. In leaving them one leaves the only spot of ground in the subject where a perfectly fair and equal fight is possible between admirers and contemners. You like " Pickwick " or you do not, and there's an end on't. Except as regards some of the inserted stories, it is all of a piece. But this could never be said again of any of the author's later works. I am not old enough to have been contemporary, at least in a state of intelligence, with any of the greater of these as they are generally reckoned. I do, indeed, remember seeing the parts of " Bleak House " in the booksellers' windows; but I did not read it till long after. I remember distinctly failing to appreciate " Hard Times," which I think rather better of now; and " A Tale of Two Cities," which I like worse every time I manage to read it. Of " Great Expectations "

I thought as a boy, and I think as a man, much better than most people did, or I believe do; and though I cannot believe that we lost much by the non-completion of " Edwin Drood," there is no doubt " the true Dickens " in parts of " Our Mutual Friend." But for that true Dickens in its quiddity we must no doubt look farther back even than "Bleak House." He achieved indeed in the latter days with Louisa and Estella something more like live girls than the wax models which under the names of Rose Maylie and Kate Nickleby, and so forth, he had been contented to exhibit in the earlier. The life philosophy of " Great Expectations," though not very extensive or thorough, is the sanest and the truest he has expressed. The dreary mannerism which appears in " Bleak House," which simply floods "Little Dorrit" and "Hard Times," and which seldom retires for long in any of the later books, is relieved by Mr. Guppy and his friends, by Affery Flintwinch, by Jo Gargery and by Herbert Pocket, by the dolls' dressmaker, by a dozen other persons and a thousand or a myriad touches and flashes. But when we think of Dickens and do not think of "Pick-wick" only, we do not think of these. It was in the forties and earliest fifties that he made his fame with "Nickleby" and "The Old Curios-ity Shop," with "Barnaby Rudge" and "Martin Chuzzlewit," with "Copperfield" and "Dom-bey," and it is with these that he must keep or lose it.

And yet how difficult it is to arrive at any settled and connected view, much more at any view that shall command anything like a general assent about even these books! In looking, for instance, for a date just now, I found in a most respectable book of reference the statement that "Agnes is perhaps the most charming character in the whole range of fiction." *Agnes!* No decent violence of expletive, no reasonable arti-fice of typography, could express the depths of my feelings at such a suggestion. It is an ob-servation almost too hackneyed to be repeated that our fathers thought Little Nell and Lit-tle Paul almost excruciatingly pathetic, while the whole of my own generation has chiefly yawned over them. I am told that the weeping time is coming again soon; but this I take leave to doubt. As a terrorist and a manufacturer of Villains with a capital V, Dickens has I believe from the first been exposed to the doubts and sneers of callous heretics. Marks and Ralph Nickleby, Barnaby Rudge's rather incomprehensible and very murderous father, Jonas Chuzzlewit, Carker the impossible, have never had the first good fortune of Paul and Nell, though they have fully shared their later decadence.

And the case of the novelist's social satire is not very different. Dickens was so essentially the middle-class Englishman of his own generation *plus* genius, that he could not fail to carry great numbers of his readers with him in his onslaughts on workhouses and public offices, on Chancery and the manufacturing system. But some at least of those readers would have been abnormally stupid if they had not perceived from the first the exaggeration and the one-sidedness which pervaded these attacks, and the astonishingly vague and unpractical character of the optimism which inspired such alternatives as the novelist suggested or seemed to suggest. Reading in parts might obscure the frequent incoherence and improbability of the stories. But except among those readers who had themselves no more knowledge of the subject than their author, it was impossible that many, even from the first, should not be struck with the almost inconceivable ignorance of all the upper and a large part of the middle class of society which his books displayed. The so-called lower classes and part of the shop-keeper rank he knew, as the French say, "like his hand." Of actors he could tell and of attorneys, and he knew a barrister in court, though hardly out of it. But his soldiers, I mean his soldier-officers, his clergymen, his scholars, his miscellaneous gentlemen, much more his baronets and his peers, were like nothing that lives and moves on any part of the earth except the boards of the stage. And so from the very earliest times there was dissidence about him, dissidence from which I must if I can in another paper endeavour, if not to extract some argument, at any rate to make clear my own view.

XIV.

DICKENS (*concluded*).

I REMEMBER reading a good many years ago, in a description (doubtless intended to be sarcastic) of an academic critic by a critic who was not academic, the item, " He likes the fun of Dickens." A person who only "liked the fun of Dickens," it was hinted (indeed I am not sure that it was not subsequently inculcated explicitly), was a nasty cynic, a superfine and unsympathetic disdainer of pathos and popular sentiment. I am afraid that I underlay then, and must still underlie, the ban of this condemnation. I should indeed not be disposed to deny now that Dickens has other claims besides mere fun. I say " now," because there was a period when I was younger and more unbalanced in judgment, and when, reserving appreciation of " Pickwick " and the Pickwickian parts

of its fellows, I was disposed to place their author unduly low. At this period I once sold a
complete set of the paper-bound issue of the
works which came out in the late sixties for half
a crown, — ostensibly and to some extent really
as a testimony of opinion as to the literary
value of the matter. This was fantastic, if not
positively foolish; but it was even at the time
not quite sincere, and such sincerity as there
was in it vanished very soon.

What may be said, I think with perfect critical truth, about Dickens is, that although he has
a good deal besides "his fun," nothing that he
has is of unalloyed excellence except that fun.
I have seen him praised for wit; but I should
say that when he is really funny he is always
humourous, but never witty. When he attempts
wit it is apt to land him in the dreary regions of
the Circumlocution Office and other dry places
wherein an over-strained satire prowls and barks.
But in his own region of partly observed, partly
exaggerated humour of the fantastic kind, his
felicity is astonishing. Although his subjects
are often technically "low" enough in all con-

science, he never here deserves the epithet "vulgar" from those who know how to use that dangerous adjective. It is only when he approaches the delineation of gentility or attempts the attitude of philosophic satire that he exhibits traces of the one unpardonable thing; and his vulgarest book, his one book tainted with incurable and hopeless vulgarity, is his "Child's History of England."

But though this terrible fault — a fault awkward to speak of inasmuch as the mere mention of it infuriates those who do not themselves feel its presence — does exist in Dickens to a most unpleasant extent, the strange alloy which, as has been noted, pervades all his work except that in pure fantastic humour, is by no means wholly due to it. The cause thereof, however, is perhaps something which aggravated his vulgarity, to wit, his unfortunate want of early education and training except of the most haphazard and self-helping kind. He appears to have been, as an editor, an extremely severe critic of other men's work, and he certainly did not take his own lightly. Yet he seems to have

9

been more destitute of the faculty of self-criticism than any person of whom I can think who
possessed anything like his powers of creation.
It is evident from the storm passage in "David
Copperfield," and some others, that he was quite
capable of writing a kind of half sober, half
ornate, and distinctly old-fashioned style, which
has very considerable merit and is not justly
exposed to any reproach on the score of taw-
driness, want of elegance, or absence of proportion.   Yet for once that he will content himself
with this, he will indulge a score of times in a
kind of trumpery strained melodramatic rant,
which is as little impressive, as completely disgusting, as the antics of a North Asian or North
American sorcerer.   He will spoil the admirable
vigour of his descriptive faculty at crises by
plastering and daubing this rant over the scenes,
and change a shudder to a yawn by simply
overdoing it.   It is this inability to know where
to stop which in like fashion has brought dis-
credit on his pathos.   He really had pathos;
but he could not be content with a moderate
dose of it, and must needs froth and whip and

be-devil it till it becomes half insipid, half ful-
some. Just the same, again, may be said of his
mere mannerisms of style and figure, though it
is fair to allow that in his very last years, unless
we may suspect a probable relapse in "Edwin
Drood," he made a rather remarkable recovery
from the depths to which he had fallen in "Little
Dorrit" and "Hard Times." In these the damnable iteration about Panks the "tug," and the
figure of Louisa as Mrs. Sparsit sees it going
down the descent, and other similar things, are
almost enough to make the gorge rise. In his
political and social satire, in his amiable optimist
life-philosophy, in his marvellous egotism, in a
dozen other characteristics of his, this same
utter absence of the sense of limit appears,
and is the secret of his failures. He will put
on the stage a clumsy lay figure like Sir John
Chester and a perfectly human being like Mrs.
Varden with equal composure, and with an
equally undoubting faith that both are quite
as they should be.

There are, I believe, some people who would
extend this unreality even to his humorous crea-

tions.   I cannot do this.   Of course in his later
years the stream naturally ran with a good
deal less of volume and with somewhat less
sparkle and sprightliness than it showed at first.
But I, at least, can discover no very great decline
in strict quality between Mr. Jingle and the
dolls' dressmaker's papa, between Dick Swivel-
ler and Joe Gargery.   There may be something
of the " irreparable outrage of years " in the
later figures, but they are of one kith and one
kin with the earlier.   No doubt such things as
the machinations of Mr. Boffin, and the exclama-
tions he utters in the effort to carry them through,
are inexpressibly tedious and dull.   But then it
is a grave error to class these with the efforts of
Dickens's own native humour at all.   They belong
to the Panks business noticed above, — to the
strange, mechanical, wooden-legged method of
dot-and-go-one progression with which he chose
at all times to alternate the easy flight of his natural wings.   They belong to the false Dickens,
the black horseman, the Mr. Hyde of the organ
ism, as distinctly as do the Markses and the
Ralph Nicklebys, the washy pathetics and the

windy politics, the leather-and-prunella peers,
and the good-young-person heroines.

It is quite different with the group, or rather
army, of immortal grotesques, who, with the
elder Mr. Weller for their general, and his son
for chief of the staff, have now travelled the
Journey from this World to the Next for a good
many years, and are, I think, tolerably safe of
their journey's end. Although, or because,
extravagance is of their essence, we seldom —
I hardly ever — feel them to be extravagant.
So unerring has been the genius of their author,
so perfectly has he arranged them in the particular key to which they belong, that the jars and
false notes which alone could throw them out
never occur. It is true, and is perhaps a necessary complement and corollary of this other
truth, that they are never completely human.
They have admirably human traits, they utter
the wisest saws and the most modern instances,
the touches of nature which their author gives
them and which they exhibit are of the finest.
Certainly they are not inhuman, but they are, I
think, decidedly extra-human. They belong to

a world not much, but definitely and unmistak-
ably, different from the actual. It has been
pointed out before now that the two great contemporaries, Dickens and Balzac, each possessed
this singular gift as it may be called from one
point of view, this singular failing as it may be
called from another. They both draw with
unerring faithfulness characters which they have
themselves invented; they fill a universe which
they have themselves created. The creation of
Dickens is indeed somewhat fantastic and shadowy beside that of Balzac, a magic lantern show
rather than a human comedy; but, on the other
hand, individual figures of the English master's
have a vividness and vigour of life exceeding
anything in the French. Yet in Dickens, even
more than in Balzac, we feel the constant presence of the theatre,— of the boards and the
lamps,— the property man and the prompter.
Take, for instance, the guests of the immortal
"Swarry" in "Pickwick," one of the greatest and
liveliest things that Dickens has done. They
have the most delightful touches; they act their
parts with remarkable *verve;* and yet we feel

that they are not real footmen. None of them
— nobody at all like them — ever opened a door
to us or took away a coat from us. Whereas
Thackeray with much less elaborate effort has
created more than one of their brethren,— J. J.'s
papa, the precious footman of Sir Francis Clav-
ering who objected to and avoided a "holterca-
tion," and others — whom we know to have been
— to be — alive. They are hanging on behind
carriages at actual drawing-rooms, and carrying
with or without a sense of offended dignity
actual coals to real fires. Those about Mr.
John Smauker never did anything of the sort
except in the Theatre Royal, Kennaquhair.

Yet this, as it seems to me, has a certain
advantage. I was surprised to see it suggested
the other day that "Pickwick" is losing its propriety of atmosphere. I should have thought
that, except to the very oldest men now living,
it had long lost all that it ever had. I am not
young, and, as I have said, I began to read
"Pickwick" very early. But, by that time, the
coaches and the hackney coaches, the domestic
suppers and the London taverns that were not

mere gin palaces, were things of the past. Nor
even when they were not can I think that " to
close observers" Dickens can ever have seemed
a realist. He was too glaringly fantastic, phan-
tasmagoric, theatrical, for that. Save in a few
externals and in his politics, which, thank
Heaven, hardly appear in " Pickwick " itself at all,
he is of no particular time, though his knowledge
of part of human nature is enough to make
him sufficiently of all. His peculiar variety of
humour has often been described as, or attributed to, animal spirits. This does not seem to
me fully adequate, for there is something much
more than mere animal spirits therein. There is
a quaint and fantastic habit of brain, an immense
observation of the ways of men, even a certain
though a limited sense of the irony of life. And
the zest and character of this are perhaps heightened by the exclusions and the short-comings
which accompany it. There is no sense of
poetry, none of mystery, hardly any of religion,
in Dickens. Passion has a merely rudimentary
and infantile expression; art and literature next
to none; philosophy none at all; history, sci-

ence, many other things, hardly any. And perhaps these lacks, these absences, helped to concentrate the force and presence of what is present, so as to intensify its marvellous humoristic quality.

XV.

MATTHEW ARNOLD.

AMONG the subjects of these papers there
is hardly one in regard to whom I can
speak in the tone of "How it struck a contemporary," to the same extent as I can with
regard to Mr. Matthew Arnold. Not of course
that I can claim to have been a contemporary
of Mr. Arnold's in the strict sense; for he had
taken his degree before I was born, and was
an author before I was able to spell. But I
can lay claim to having seen the birth of his
popularity, its whole career till his death, the
stationary state which preceded and succeeded
that death, and something like a commencement
of the usual depreciation and spoliation which
so surely follows. For Mr. Arnold's reputation
made no very early or general way with the
public, however high it may have been with his
private friends, and with a small circle of (chiefly

University) readers of poetry. A University Professorship has not very often been the occasion of attracting public attention to a man in England; but it may be said with some confidence that the remarkable " Lectures on Translating Homer" were the first which drew to Mr. Arnold the notice of the world. He was then nearly forty, and he was several years over that Age of Wisdom when the " French Eton " and still more the " Essays in Criticism " fascinated the public with a double mannerism of speech and thought in prose, and set it inquiring about the author's verse.

Most young men of twenty who had any taste for English letters when the " Essays " appeared fell in love with them, I believe, at once and desperately, with the more or less natural consequence of getting tired of them, if not positively disliking them, afterwards. My own admiration for them was, to the best of my remembrance, a good deal more lukewarm at first; and though it has never got any colder since, and has, I think, a little increased in temperature, it never has been, and I do not think

it ever will be, at boiling point. I may give
some reasons for this later, for the moment let
us be historical.

It was undoubtedly one of those happy coin-
cidences which, according to the optimist, happen to all of us who really deserve them, that
just after the reading public had awakened to
the sense that there was a very piquant and remarkable writer of English prose wrapped in
the coat of one whom it had hitherto regarded,
if at all, as a composer of elegant, but rather
academic verse, the great political change of
1867 happened, and a reign of sharp social and
political changes began. I do not think myself
that the revolution of 1868–1874 has ever been
fully estimated, and I have always thought
it half an advantage and half a disadvantage
that I was myself resident out of London during
the whole of that time. The looker-on sees the
drift of the game more clearly, but he appre-
ciates the motives and aims of those who take
part in it less fully than the players. During
these years Mr. Arnold seemed to have a great
part before him. Everything (following his

father's famous definition of Liberalism) "was
an open question," and the Apostle of Culture
with his bland conviction, first, that most things
were wrong in England, and, secondly, that he
was born to set them right, and with a singu-
larly stimulating and piquant style to help him,
had an unusually clear field.

As a matter of fact, Mr. Arnold did help to
produce a considerable effect on the public.
But it was an effect chiefly negative as far as
the public was concerned, and it cannot be said
to have been altogether happy as regards himself. To the finest flowers of his production,
such as the delightful whimsy of "Friendship's
God," little attention was paid : the good public, Populace, Philistines, and Barbarians alike,
could not make out what the devil Mr. Arnold
was driving at. His formulas, after pleasing for
a while, were seen to be rather empty things;
his actual politics, if he had any, (a point on
which I have always entertained doubts,) appeared to be totally unpractical; and he had not
the chance which Mr. Mill and Mr. Morley en-
joyed or suffered, of showing whether a sojourn

in the House could practicalise them. Un-
luckily too for him, he allowed his energies to
drift almost wholly into the strange anti-theological kind of theology which occupied him for
nearly ten years, which at first brought on him
much odium and never attained for him much
reputation, which appears to me, I confess, to
have palpably stiffened and dulled his once marvellous lissomeness and brilliancy of thought,
and which is now abandoned to cheap beginners
in undogmatism alike by the orthodox and the
unorthodox of some mental calibre.

Then for another ten years Mr. Arnold settled
slowly back again, under the disadvantages just
referred to, into his proper line of poet, literary
and miscellaneous essayist, and mild satirist of
society. Once in verse, in the exquisite lines
entitled "Westminster Abbey" (I would they
had had a better subject, not than the Abbey,
but than Dean Stanley), once or twice in prose,
as in the famous charge on the Shelleyites and
other things, the Apostle of Sweetness and
Light appeared at his very best; and perhaps
he was never, except in the wondrous muddle-

headedness of the "Irish Essays," far below it.
But in all the works of this time, though the
positive dulness of the phase of which "St.
Paul and Protestantism" is perhaps the Nadir
never reappeared, there is, to me at least, a sense
of two drawbacks. There is a failing *fineness* of
power in a man whose power had at its best
been nothing if not fine, a growing heaviness
of touch, a sleight of words that becomes a
trick, a damnable iteration, an occasional passage from agreeable impertinence to something
else that is not agreeable. And there is, on the
other hand, an obvious disgust and dissatisfac-
tion at the very results which he had hoped and
helped to attain. It was impossible that Mr.
Arnold should accept democracy with anything
but the wryest of faces; and he must have found
the new Pharisees of undogmatism whom his
religious musings had brought about suggestive
of another work by the same author as "Religious Musings,"—the "Ode to a Young Ass."
The Young Ass has begun to kick at Mr.
Arnold now, I see, as the fashion of him passeth
away.

But it was never possible for any competent person, however much he might find to dislike in this fascinating and irritating writer, to fail in recognition of his extraordinary powers. One might wince at the almost unbelievable faults of taste which he, *arbiter elegantiarum* as he was, would not unfrequently commit; frown at the gaudy tricks of a mannerism quite as bad as those which he was never weary of denouncing; demur to his misleading and snip-snap phrases about "criticism of life," "lucidity," "grand style," and what not. There were a great many things that he did not know or did not fancy; and like most of us, no doubt, he was very apt to think that what he did not know was not worth the knowing, and that only very poor and unhappy creatures could like what he did not fancy.

Now all these things are specially bad preparations for the task of the critic; and perhaps Mr. Arnold's critical abilities, if not overrated, were wrongly estimated. It was difficult to praise too highly the expression of his criticism when it was at its best; but it was easy to

set the substance too high. Even his subtlety
and his acuteness, two faculties in regard to
which I suppose his admirers would put him
highest, were rather more apparent than real,
and were constantly blunted and fettered by the
extraordinary narrowness and crotchettiness of
his range of sympathies. He was always
stumbling over his own formulas; and he not
unfrequently violated his own canons. At least
I am myself quite unable to reconcile that doctrine of confining ourselves to " the best," which
it seems rules out the " Chanson de Roland "
and makes Shelley more remarkable as a let-
ter-writer than as a poet, with the attention
paid to Sénancour and the Guérins.

The real value of Mr. Arnold as a critic —
apart from his indirect merit of providing much
delightful English prose shot with wit and
humour, and enclosing endless sweetmeats if
not solids of sense — consisted chiefly in the
comparative novelty of the style of literary
appreciation which he adopted, and in the stimu-
lus which he accordingly gave to literary study.
Since Hazlitt, we had been deficient in critics

10

who put appreciation before codification; and
Hazlitt himself was notoriously untrustworthy
through caprice. The following of Sainte-Beuve
saved Mr. Arnold from both errors to some
extent, but to some extent only. Though well
read, he was not extremely learned; and though
acute, he was the very reverse of judicial. He
had fortunately been brought up on classical
literature, to which he pinned his faith; and it
is impossible that any one with this advantage
should be a literary heretic of the worst description. But he constantly committed the fault
of Shylock in regard to his classics. What was
not in the classical bond, what "was not so
expressed," could not be good, could not at
least be of the best. Now I will yield to no
man in my respect for the classics; and I do
not think that, at least as far as the Greeks are
concerned, any one will ever do better the
things that they did. But it is absurd to suppose or maintain that the canon of literary
perfections was closed when the Muses left
Philemon's house.

Mr. Arnold, then, as a critic seemed to me

at first, and has always seemed to me, flawed
with these very faults of freak and crotchet
against which he was never tired of protesting, and, though a very useful alterative-stim-
ulant, and check, not a good model, and a still
worse oracle. I should say of him, and I
think I have always recked my own rede from
1865 to the present day in this respect, "Admire, enjoy, and be thankful for Mr. Arnold as
a critic; but be careful about imitating him,
and never obey him without examination."
Of Mr. Arnold as a poet there is much more
to be said.

XVI.

MATTHEW ARNOLD (*concluded*).

THE book in which I first made acquaintance with any considerable quantity of Mr. Arnold's poetry was the so-called second edition of the "Poems," containing the first issue of the celebrated Preface: perhaps the best piece of criticism (though I do not agree with its main position) that the author ever did. The book in which one has first made full acquaintance with a poet is like no other book; it has the charm of one of the two kisses celebrated by the Spanish folk-song. Yet I venture to think — divorcing criticism as much as possible from any pathetic or egotistic fallacy — that the collection was and is an extremely favourable one for the purpose of doing full but friendly justice to Mr. Arnold's poetical talent. For it was the selected collection of a good deal of separately written and

XVII.

THREE MID–CENTURY NOVELISTS.

CHARLOTTE BRONTE. — GEORGE ELIOT. — ANTHONY TROLLOPE.

THERE are, I suppose, no Victorian novelists, putting very recent names with whom I do not here meddle out of the question, who have approached the popularity of Dickens and Thackeray more nearly than Charlotte Bronte, George Eliot, and Anthony Trollope. They are at the present moment in three different stages of the experience which popular novelists go through when they die, and it may be a little interesting to examine their case from the point of view of the present papers.

The author of " Jane Eyre " has had one indisputable reward for the shortness of her brilliant career. She has become a classic; she has been recently reprinted as such with authors the youngest of whom was her senior by nearly half a century; and though it cannot be said that she had ever quite fallen out of even popular knowledge, any one with a tolerably sharp eye for criticism must have perceived that not a few readers come to her, as they come to a classic, with a more or less respectful ignorance. She was protected from that most ungracious stage of depreciation which attacks many of her kind immediately after, if not even before, their death, first by the earliness of that event in her case, and secondly by the fact that it happened at a peculiar period. In 1855 the English world had not yet become literary; and though I do not know that the quality of the best literary criticism was much better or much worse than it is now, the volume of it was infinitely smaller. There were far fewer newspapers; and the young person who, on the strength of a modern education, a comfortable confidence in his own judgment, and a hand-book or two of authorities quotable and pillageable, commences critic, existed in smaller numbers, and had very much fewer openings. Moreover, Currer Bell had held one of those literary positions which expose the holder to more hardships at first than afterwards. She belonged to no school; she was not involved in any literary parties; she rose with few rivals, and she died before she had time to create any. So that, though she had great difficulties in making her way, and was subjected to some unfair and ungenerous comments at first, when she had begun to make that way she had little direct detraction to fear.

I do not think that she was exactly what can be called a great genius, or that she would ever have given us anything much better than she did give; and I do not think that with critical reading "Jane Eyre" improves, or even holds its ground very well. It has strength, or at any rate force; it has sufficient originality of manner; it has some direct observation of life within the due limits of art; and it has the piquancy of an unfashionable unconventionality at a very conventional time. These are good things, but they are not necessarily great; and it is to me a very suspicious point that quite the best parts of Charlotte Bronte's work are admittedly

something like transcripts of her personal experience. It is very good to be able to record
personal experience in this pointed and vivid
way; and perhaps few great creators, if any,
have been independent of personal experience.
But they have for the most part transcribed it
very far off; and they have intermixed the tran-
scription with a far larger amount of direct observation of others, and of direct imagination or
creation. Those who have not done so fall into
the second or lower place, and do not often rise
out of it. This is an experience for confirmation of which I can, I think, confidently appeal
to all competent reviewers and most competent
editors. A book appears, or an article is sent
in, wherein this or that incident, mood, character, what not, is treated with distinct vigour and
freshness. The reviewer praises, and looks with
languid interest tempered by sad experience for
the second book; the editor accepts, and looks
with eagerness tempered by experience still
more fatal for the second article. Both come,
and lo! there is either a distinct falling off from,
or a total absence of, the first fine rapture. I

think Charlotte Bronte is the capital example
of this familiar fact, in a person who has actually
attained to literature.

Not that she never did anything good after
" Jane Eyre." I think better than most people
seem to have done of " Shirley," somewhat less
well perhaps of " Villette " and " The Professor."
But in all, from " Jane Eyre " itself downward,
there is that rather fatal note of the presence
and apparent necessity of the personal experience. It is portrait painting or *genre*, not crea-
tive art of the unmistakable kind, and in the one
case where there seems to be a certain projec-
tion of the ideal, the egregious Mr. Rochester,
even contemporary opinion — thankful as it was
for a variation of type from the usual hero with
the chiselled nose, the impeccable, or, if pecca-
ble, amiable character, and the general nullity
— recognised at once that the ideal was rather
a poor one. It was as much of a schoolgirl's or
a governess's hero as any one of Scott's or
Byron's. It is quite true that Rochester is not
merely ugly and rude, but his ugliness and his
rudeness are so much of him! And though

Jane herself is much more than an underbred little hussy, I fear there is underbreeding and hussyness in her, where she is not a mere photograph. I used to think, years ago, that the finest touch in all Miss Bronte's work is where the boy in "Shirley" makes up his mind to ask Caroline for a kiss as the price of his services, and does not. I am not much otherwise minded now.

———◆———

Twenty years ago it required, if not a genuine strength of mind, at any rate a certain amount of "cussedness," not to be a George-Eliotite. All, or almost all, persons who had "got culture" admired George Eliot, and not to do so was to be at best a Kenite among the chosen people, at worst an outcast, a son of Edom and Moab and Philistia. Two very different currents met and mingled among the worshippers who flocked in the flesh to St. John's Wood, or read the books in ecstasy elsewhere. There was the rising tide of the æsthetic, revering the creator of Tito. There was the agnostic herd, faithful to the translator of Strauss and the

irregular partner of Mr. G. H. Lewes.   I have
always found myself most unfortunately indis-
posed to follow any fashion, and I never remember having read a single book of George
Eliot's with genuine and whole-hearted admiration.   Yet an experience which I once went
through enables me, I think, to speak about
her at least without ignorance.   When "Daniel
Deronda" appeared, my friend, the late Dr.
Appleton, asked me to review it for the *Acad-
emy*.   My hands were the reverse of full at
the time, and as there were some books of the
author's which I had not read, and others which
I had not read for some time, I thought it might
be worth while to get an entire set and read it
through in chronological order, and so "get the
atmosphere" before attacking that Ebrew Jew.
I have spent many days with less pleasure and
less profit than those which I spent on this task.
And when I had finished it, I came to an opinion
which I have since seen little reason to change.

Something of what has been already said
about Charlotte Bronte will apply also to this
very different contemporary and craftsfellow of

hers. Neither of them seems to have had in any great degree the male faculties of creation and judgment. Both, and Miss Evans especially, had in no ordinary degree the female faculty of receiving, assimilating, and reproducing. During a long and studious youth she received and assimilated impressions of persons, of scenes, of books. At a rather belated crisis of feeling she experienced what I suppose must be called Love, and at the same time was exposed to a fresh current of thought, such as it was. She travelled and enriched her store; she frequented persons of distinction and was influenced by them. And then it came out in novels, at first pretty simple, and really powerful; then less simple, but ingeniously reproductive of certain phases of thought and sentiment which were current; last of all reflective of hardly anything (save in scattered and separate scenes where she always excelled) except strange crotchets of will-worship, which she had taken up to replace the faith that she had cast out, but that was evidently more or less necessary to her.

She began with those "Scenes of Clerical

Life," which some very fervent worshippers of hers, I believe, put at the head of all her work in merit as in time, but which I should rank decidedly below the best parts of " Adam Bede " and the wonderful opening of " Silas Marner." Then came the great triumph, " Adam Bede," itself. Of course it is extremely clever ; but no one who calls himself a critic can afford to forget the circumstances in which it appeared. Dickens's best work was done, and his mannerism was already disgusting some readers. Thackeray, though at his very best, had not reached full popularity, and was entirely different in style and subject. Charlotte Bronte was dead or dying, — I forget which ; there was nobody else who could even pretend to the first class. How could " Adam Bede " fail?

"The Mill on the Floss " was not likely, the circumstances being still the same, to diminish the author's vogue, and I suppose it is her best book, though it may not contain her best scenes. The objection which is often made and still oftener felt to the repulsiveness of Maggie's worship of a counter-jumping cad like Stephen, is somewhat uncritical. I suspect that most women resent it, because they feel the imputation to be true : and most men out of a not wholly dissimilar feeling which acts a little differently. "Silas Marner" again has qualities of greatness, though the narrative and characters are slight for a book. But between these earlier novels and the later batch a great gulf is fixed. Hardly after "Silas" do we find anything, except in patches and episodes, that is really "genial" in George Eliot's work. "Felix Holt" and "Middlemarch" are elaborate studies of what seemed to the author to be modern characters and society,— studies of immense effort and erudition not unenlightened by humour, but on the whole dead. "Romola" is an attempt — still more Herculean, and still more against the grain — to resuscitate the past. As for "Daniel Deronda," it is a kind of nightmare, — a parochial and grotesque idea having thoroughly mastered the writer and only allowed her now and then to get free in the character of Grandcourt and (less often) in that of Gwendolen. I think "Theophrastus Such" has met with rather undeserved contempt, due to the fact that "Deronda" had already begun to sap the foundations of its author's popularity. The poems are laboured and thoroughly unpoetical expositions of crotchet and theory. The essays are neither better nor worse than a vast number of essays by quite second-rate authors.

I must collect, in the old sense, the results of this in another paper, which will also give me room to speak of Mr. Trollope.

XVIII.

THREE MID–CENTURY NOVELISTS
(*concluded*).

THE brief sketch of the history of George
Eliot's work from the outside which was
given at the end of the last paper might almost
carry with it, to a wary and experienced mind,
a forecast of the progress of George Eliot's
reputation. But there was another influence
of the first importance which has not yet been
noticed. I never knew anything personally of
Mr. G. H. Lewes. But he was certainly a very
clever man: and as a literary trainer, with a view
to the present success of the still more clever
companion whom accident threw in his way, he
was really consummate. I think George Eliot
might possibly have occupied a higher place in
literary history if she had never met him at all;
but it is rather more probable that she might
have occupied none whatever. As it was, he

managed to put her literary faculties in a kind
of forcing-house. The anonymity which was
maintained over the "Scenes of Clerical Life"
and "Adam Bede," may have been at first unintentional, but its effect both on the public and
the producer was no doubt stimulating in the
highest degree. When it had been dropped,
Mr. Lewes fell at once with extraordinary tact
into the way of life which best suited the forte
and the foible of Miss Evans. He gave her
assiduous personal attention and a sort of sham
position as the head of a family. He did not
overwork her, and he administered plenty of the
foreign travel and home atmosphere of literary
society which she liked. He fended off all but
favourable reviews, and while dexterously sur-
rounding her with a court of faithful devotees
protected her from any rough contact with the
give-and-take of the world. All these things
worked together with her own unquestioned
endowments, not merely to bring her money
and fame, but actually to stimulate her productive faculties to the highest possible point
in a certain way.

In a certain other way the result was disas-
trous. She never lived in the open. Her first
intellectual expansion had taken place in a narrow clique of Unitarian Nonconformity; and she
had but exchanged it for one little wider, of
agnostic and anti-theological journalism. Her
last twenty or five and twenty years were spent
in a close conservatory, receiving adulation from
others, and brooding over her own negative
creed. The nearest analogue that I can think
of to her among the greater names of fiction is
Richardson, to whose work hers has indeed a
striking resemblance in more ways than one.
But even Richardson lived in a healthier time
and was exposed to healthier influences. Nobody "rattled her shutters," to take Thackeray's excellent metaphor, as Fielding rattled
Richardson's. She had no experience of active
business, such as the printer had, with ruthless
customers, prosaic workmen, and the like, to give
her a taste of the actual world. And so there
was, even from the first, a taint of the morbid
and the unnatural upon her. The flowers forced
from her in this non-natural atmosphere and by

this non-natural treatment had, as is customary in such cases, no small *éclat* and attraction at first, but their colour and their form grew less and less lifelike as time went on, and their inherent weakness caused them to fade sooner and sooner. That this would have been the case anyhow I do not doubt, but the Nemesis of the *liaison* with Lewes exhibited itself in an even more unmistakable fashion than this. The scientific phraseology to which he himself was more or less sincerely devoted invaded his companion's writing with a positive contagion, and what many independent critics had been saying for years became the public voice on the appearance of " Daniel Deronda." Coterie admiration lasted a little longer; and that popular reflex which a well-engineered fame always brings with it, a little longer still. And then it all broke down, and for some years past George Eliot, though she may still be read, has more or less passed out of contemporary critical appreciation. There are, of course, a few obstinate and " know-nothing " worshippers; perhaps there are some who kept their heads even in the heyday, and who can now say *sunt lachrymæ rerum*, as they contemplate a fame once so great, in part so solidly founded, and yet now to a greater extent than strict justice can approve almost utterly vanished away.

———◆———

The vicissitudes of Mr. Anthony Trollope's reputation are less striking and perhaps less instructive than those of George Eliot's, for there can be very little doubt that Miss Evans had genius, and I never met more than one competent critic (a personal friend, by the way, of the author of "The Warden") who thought that Mr. Trollope had. But he had immense fertility, and if not immense, very great talent; and his career is in consequence something of a warning. Unless I mistake very greatly, no novelist towards the end of the sixties was in greater demand at the circulating libraries, and by the editors and publishers of magazines which published serial novels, than Mr. Trollope; and certainly no one ever set himself to satisfy that demand with greater energy or in a more business-like spirit.

He probably did himself no good with the public or the critics by the quaint frankness of his avowals in his Autobiography as to the strictly professional fashion — so many hours per day, and so many words per hour — in which he did his "chores." And certainly there was a time when the public altogether failed to respond to his endeavours to please them. His last half-dozen, if not his last dozen novels, were I believe indifferent pecuniary successes; and I remember very well the difficulties under which I found myself when I had to criticise more than one of them. For it is, I think, a law of the Medes and Persians, "Never speak evil of man or woman who has given you pleasure," and I admit that in the days of the "Chronicles of Barset," Mr. Trollope gave me a very great deal of pleasure. But it is also a law of honest criticism never to say what you do not think, though it is by no means necessary to say all that you do think, and it was not easy to reconcile these two laws in the late seventies and early eighties with regard to Mr. Anthony Trollope.

He seems indeed to me to be the most remark-

able example we have yet seen of a kind of writer
who I suppose is destined to multiply as long as
the fancy for novel-reading lasts.   Only a few
months ago it fell to my lot to read through the
work of a famous *amuseur* of this kind in the generation before Mr. Trollope's, a man as famous
as himself in his own day, and of gifts certainly
more varied and perhaps not less considerable.
And the resemblance between Theodore Hook
and Anthony Trollope struck me, I own, forcibly
and rather terribly.   Hook is of course at a
much greater disadvantage with a reader of the
present day — at least with a reader of my standing — than is Trollope.   Much of him is positively obsolete, while in Trollope's case the
mere outward framework, the ways and language
of society, the institutions, customs, and atmosphere of daily life, have not had time to alter
very strikingly, if at all.   Trollope too, did not
attempt the purely comic vein, as did Hook;
and the purely comic vein, unless it be absolutely
transcendent, and of the first class, is that which
dries soonest.

But still they are of the same general kind,

and their motto, the motto of their kind, is *Mene, Tekel*.   I do not even think that any one is ever again likely to attain even so high a rank in it as Mr. Trollope's.   Most have got the seed, and the flower has become common accordingly.   I do not know that I myself ever took Mr. Trollope for one of the immortals; but really between 1860 and 1870 it might have been excusable so to take him.   In "Barchester Towers," especially, there are characters and scenes which go uncommonly near the characters and scenes that do not die.   Years later the figure of Mr. Crawley and the scene of the final vanquishing of Mrs. Proudie simulate, if they do not possess, immortal quality.   And in the enormous range of the other books earlier and later it would not be difficult to single out a number — a very considerable number — of passages not greatly inferior to these.   From almost the beginning until quite the end, Mr. Trollope — whether by diligent contemplation of models, by dexterous study from the life, or by the mere persistent craftsman's practice which turns out pots till it turns them out flawlessly — showed the faculty

of constructing a thoroughly readable story.
You might not be extraordinarily enamoured
of it; you might not care to read it again; you
could certainly feel no enthusiastic reverence
for or gratitude to its author. But it was emi-
nently satisfactory; it was exactly what it held
itself out to be; it was just what men and
women had sent to Mudie's to get. Perhaps
there is never likely to be very much, and still
less likely to be too much, of such work about
the world.

And yet even such work is doomed to pass,
— with everything that is of the day and the
craftsman, not of eternity and art. It was
not because Mr. Trollope had, as I believe he
had in private life, a good deal of the genial
Philistine about him, that his work lacks the
certain vital signs. We have record of too
many artists, up to the very greatest, who took
no romantic or sacerdotal view of their art, and
who met the demand of the moment as regu-
larly and peaceably as might be. You will no
more avoid failure by systematic unbusiness-
likeness, than you will secure success by strict

attention to business.   The fault of the Trollopian novel is in the quality of the Trollopian
art.   It is shrewd, competent, not insufficiently
supported by observation, not deficient in more
than respectable expressive power, careful, in-
dustrious, active enough.   But it never has the
last exalting touch of genius, it is every-day,
commonplace, and even not infrequently vulgar.
These are the three things that great art never
is; though it may busy itself with far humbler
persons and objects than Mr. Trollope does,
may confine itself even more strictly than he
does to purely ordinary occurrences, may shun
the exceptional, the bizarre, the *outré*, as rigidly
as Miss Austen herself.   Indeed, there is a very
short road to vulgarity by affecting these last
three things; and I think since Mr. Trollope's
time it has been pretty frequently trodden by
those who are hastening to the same goal of
comparative oblivion which, I fear, he has already reached.

12

XIX.

MR. WILLIAM MORRIS.

I THINK it probable that no long poem has for many years — indeed, since the disuse of buying such poems by tens of thousands in the days of our grandfathers — sold so well as "The Earthly Paradise"; and I believe that, though none of Mr. Morris's subsequent works has equalled this in popularity, they have none of them lacked a fair vogue. Yet it has always seemed to me that not merely the general, but even the critical public ranks him far below his proper station as a poet.

The way in which I made my own first acquaintance with him was very odd; and I have never been able fully to explain it. As a boy of certainly not more than fourteen I used, like other boys, to take in periodicals addressed *pueris* if not *virginibus*, and in one of these, the title of which I cannot remember, I can very

distinctly mind me of seeing an editorial notice
of a poem which had been sent in, dealing with
a " tall white maid " and other things and persons. This poem was, as I afterwards found
out, and as all Morrisians will recognize, " The
Sailing of the Sword," which must just have
appeared, or have been just about to appear, in
Mr. Morris's first volume, " The Defence of
Guinevere." This volume came out in 1858, —
an *annus mirabilis*, in which some of the best
wine of the century was made on the Douro,
and in the Gironde, and on the Côte d'Or, and
which seems to have exercised a very remarkable influence on the books and persons born
in it. The persons of 1858 had a singular knack
of being clever or charming, or both ; and the
books (as biographers and bibliographers have
before noticed) were unusually epoch-making.

Of these I do not myself rank " The Defence
of Guinevere " least high. " The Sailing of the
Sword " — the manner of the insertion of which
in my *Boys' Magazine*, or whatever it was called,
remains an insoluble mystery to me — is, no
doubt, not one of the best. But I remember

when some years afterwards I bought the little
brown book — nightingale-colour — from Slatter
and Rose's counter at Oxford for a price which
would not buy it now, that I took it back to my
rooms and read it straight through with an
ecstasy of relish not surpassed by anything
I have ever known of the kind. Persons of
sober and classical tastes fought very shy of
"Guinevere" at her first appearance; and even
some of those who loved her then have fallen
off now. Why should a man speak about a
"choosing-cloth"? What were these strange
scraps of mediæval French? Who could make
sense of "The Blue Closet" or "Two Red
Roses across the Moon"? Indeed, this latter
very harmless and spirited ditty — of which I
once offered to write a symbolic defence in any
required number of pages, and which I still love
wildly — had the faculty of simply infuriating
the grave and precise. Oxford and Cambridge
have not in my time produced better scholars,
who are also humourists, or humourists who are
also scholars, than the present Sir Frederick
Pollock and the present Bishop of Colombo,

and I believe it to be no improper revealing of
secrets to say that they both at least used to
abominate it. Perhaps (I hope so) they do not
now. As for the incident, when the orange fell
" And in came marching the ghosts of those
who were slain at the war," I should like to
bring up the men from the south gate and have
a fleet horse ready at that postern, before setting
it even now before some very respectable persons. And then it would have been more dangerous still.

For my part I loved the book at once with
a love full-grown and ardent; nor do I think
that that love has decreased an inch in stature
or a degree in heat since. Of course there
are very obvious faults and foibles. The archaic mannerism may be here and there overdone, even in the eyes of those who are well
enough inclined thereto; the attention to pictorial and to musical effect may sometimes seem
paid at the expense of sense. The title-poem
is in parts obscure and wordy; " Sir Peter
Harpdon's End," another most important piece,
would gain a great deal by cutting down; the

expression sometimes lacks crispness and finish ;
the verse is sometimes facile and lax. But all
this is redeemed and more than redeemed by
the presence of the real, the true, the indefinable and unmistakable spirit of poetry. And
this spirit wears, as it does at all its more
remarkable appearances in the world, a distinct
and novel dress. Although the so-called Romantic movement had been going on more or
less for a hundred years — had been going on
vigorously and decidedly for sixty or seventy
— when Mr. Morris wrote, only one or two
snatches of Coleridge and Keats had caught the
peculiar mediæval tone which the Præ-Raphael-
ites in poetry, following the Præ-Raphaelites in
art, were now about to sound. Even " La Belle
Dame Sans Merci," that wonderful divination
in which Keats hit upon the true and very
mediæval, as elsewhere upon the true and very
classical spirit, is an exception, a casual inspiration rather than a full reflection. And
let it be remembered that when Mr. Morris
began to write, the brother poets (who afterwards a little eclipsed him, perhaps, both with

the public and the critics) had published nothing
(though Mr. Rossetti's sugared sonnets might
be handed about among his private friends),
and that the painter who is more than any one
Mr. Morris's yoke-fellow, Sir Edward Burne-
Jones, was hardly out of leading-strings.

"The Defence of Guinevere," indeed, was not
Mr. Morris's first, not even his first published,
work.   He contributed largely to that very
remarkable and now very inaccessible miscel-
lany, *The Oxford and Cambridge Magazine*, his
chief work being, I believe, a delightful romance
called "The Hollow Land," which I read, all
unknowing its authorship, at the age of sixteen,
and liked, but not to loving. "The Hollow
Land" was, as I remember it, after more than
thirty years, a little, a very little, incoherent
and apocalyptic — with painters who painted
God's judgments in purple and crimson, and
a heroine of the appropriate name of Swan-
hilda.   I decline to recognize any real incohe-
rency in "The Defence of Guinevere."   The
whole book is, of course, saturated with the
spirit of the Arthurian legends, of which I be-

lieve Mr. Morris was even then a great student, both in French and in English. Nor do I think that any one who does not know the originals, and has not gone through a considerable study of mediæval romance, can fully estimate the marvellous manner in which he has not merely galvanized or copied, but revivified and recreated the tone and sense of them. For — the warning has often been given, but it wants repetition still — it is quite a mistake to think that either Scott earlier, or Lord Tennyson later, effected this revivification, magnificent as the work of both is. Scott was an ardent lover of the Middle Ages; but he was, after all, a man born well within the eighteenth century. Tennyson had read his Mallory faithfully; but he was not born much within the nineteenth. It took the work of these very men to create the atmosphere — to get ready the stage — in which and on which Mr. Morris and Sir Edward Burne-Jones could appear.

That stage, that atmosphere, must always, I suppose, find a public either enthusiastic in welcome or vehement in refusal. It is not easy

to be merely indifferent to the works of these
artists, though it is possible merely to gape at
them in uncomprehending wonder. "Pastiche"
will cry the one side; "unmeaning and overdone
archaism; sentimental maundering; indifference to the gains and the aims of modernism;
art too literary; literature too pictorial; illiberal
and pusillanimous relapse on a mainly imagi-
nary past; deficiency in realism; reliance on
trick and *cliché.*" I may be excused from setting in array against these terms of excessive
and uncritical depreciation a counter list of
equally excessive appreciation and praise. But
I think myself that the school in question —
especially the poet and the painter just coupled
— have discovered, or rather rediscovered, the
way to one of the Paradises of Art, of which
I shall not say much more in this place than
that to my judgment it seems a true and genuine Paradise, and, to my taste, one delicious
and refreshing to an extent not excelled by any
other. To me personally, no other division of
literature or of art has the qualities of a "Vale
of Rest" as mediæval literature and mediæval

art have; while the renaissance of both, at the hands of Mr. Morris and his friends, seems to me a true renaissance, not by any means a copy, possessing the qualities of its originals in a slightly altered and perhaps even more effective form.

It has a fashion of delight, standing in the most marked and interesting contrast with those fashions which may be noticed in other poets of the period. Like the Tennysonian charm, it is dreamlike; but the character of the dreams is distinct. There is more action, more story, in them; and at the same time there is a double and treble dose of the vague and the mystical in colour, form, and sound. In Tennyson there is still a sort of remnant of eighteenth-century *netteté*, of classical clearness of outline. It is only with Mr. Morris and his friends or followers that we get into the true Romantic vague. When Mr. Lang selected Mr. Morris as the chief English example of poetry which oversteps the border line between mere sound and sense, he did justly. But it is also necessary to take count in Mr. Morris of that extraordinarily decorative spirit which always makes him accompany his music with limning. He is the very embodiment of mediæval poetry as we meet it in the well known opening of the "Romance of the Rose" and a thousand other places, — a noise of musical instruments accompanying an endless procession of allegorical or purely descriptive imagery. Between William of Lorris and William Morris there are six hundred years of time, a single letter in spelling, and in spirit only a greater genius, the possession of a happier instrument of language, and a larger repertory of subject and style in the later singer.

XX.

MR. WILLIAM MORRIS (*concluded*).

THERE are certain of one's literary as of one's other loves the progress of which is not wholly satisfactory to a person of sensibility. There may be no actual " writing out; " no positive and undeniable deterioration; but "the second temple is not like the first," later pressures do not repeat the effect of the first sprightly runnings. I at least have never felt this with Mr. William Morris. I never met him in the flesh, or exchanged letters with him, or heard very much about him personally; and *si quid id est*, I think his politics very nearly childish, and much more than very nearly mischievous. But I know no man of letters of my time who has been so thoroughly satisfactory all through to the critical lover of letters. To the critical lover, I say advisedly. And yet it must be not quite the ordinary

sort of critic who shall do Mr. Morris full
justice. For his faults are exactly of those
which the critic who looks only at the stop-
watch will least pardon; and his merits are
perhaps of those which the critic who looks
only at the stop-watch will least appreciate.

In the last division of this paper I have given
some remarks on his work as it appeared up to
and including "The Defence of Guinevere."
His next stroke was a stroke of genius, and it
was, also, as strokes of genius are not always, a
stroke of good luck. The hubbub about Mr.
Swinburne's "Poems and Ballads" had made
general and popular what had before been only
partial and esoteric, — an interest in the new
schools of Præ-Raphaelite art and letters which
had already fixed in various ways strong holds
on the Universities, especially Oxford. But
"The Life and Death of Jason, a Poem by
William Morris, London, Bell and Daldy, 1867,"
which lies beside me with its red buckram
weathered to orange on the back, but otherwise
much as I bought it at its earliest appearance,
hit the bird on both wings. It gave a perfect

Romantic treatment.   It chose a perfect classical subject.   It was not possible, as it has been
since, for any one to accuse the artist of too
much archaic mannerism in the mediæval and
Scandinavian manner; it was not possible, on
the other side, for any one not to recognize
that here was an almost entirely new fashion
of telling a story in verse.   It was new, but
it was not ancestorless; few things are.   It
had in its genealogy not merely Keats, but
Wither and Browne.   But the result, as happens sometimes in well-bred steeds, was a
far more spirited and individual product than
any of its forbears.   Mr. Morris did to the
heroic couplet what Milton and Wordsworth
did to blank verse.   He broke it up, changed
its centres of gravity, subjected it to endless
varieties of *enjambement* or overlapping.   It
was his main care to end a paragraph, to begin a speech, in the middle of a couplet or
a line.   Yet he never was harsh, and he was
seldom — he was sometimes — over fluent.   The
thing took by storm that portion of the public
which has scholarship as well as taste.   And

it deserved to take it. I do not think myself that there is any one passage quite so exquisite in it as the "Nymph's Song to Hylas,"
which Mr. Morris (either desirous not to let
it be whelmed in a long narrative, or trying
experiments on the public memory) republished
twenty years after in "Songs by the Way." But
it is all more or less exquisite, and it was then
all more or less novel.

It was soon to be to a certain extent antiquated by a more splendid production from the
same hand. I really do not know that anything
combining bulk and excellence to the same
extent as "The Earthly Paradise" had appeared since Dryden's "Fables," and the "Fables" are but small in bulk compared to the
"Paradise."

A Paradise it certainly is. It had been her-
alded on the fly-leaves of "Jason," and again
in its own earlier volumes, not quite in the form
which it finally assumed. I have been told that
all the defaulting tales exist, and I would I had
them. For nothing is wrong in this enormous
work. If it is sometimes voluble, it is never

prosaic; the setting-pieces, intercalated prefaces,
and epilogues for the several months, are as
they should be, of the very best; the proem
is noble; and the general contents are sublime.
It is hard to seek among the two dozen for the
best where all are good. For mere personal
liking I should choose, I think, "The Man born
to be King" (which is worth comparing with
the simplicity of the old French story), "The
Doom of King Acrisius," with the gorgeous
sweep of its rendering of the Perseus legend,
"The Watching of the Falcon" (a great ser-
mon on a great text), "The Land East of the
Sun and West of the Moon" (an ideal Romantic
tale), its immediate forerunner, "The Death of
Paris" (which will bear comparison with the
early and late work of Tennyson himself), and
lastly "The Ring given to Venus" and "The
Hill of Venus," the first of which pair contains,
in the procession of the dead Gods from sea
to land, perhaps the very finest thing that Mr.
Morris has ever done. If only Sir Edward
Burne-Jones would take it for a subject!

I suppose there is no douce and reasonable

Morrisian who will deny that "The Earthly
Paradise" marks the apogee of its writer's
talent. But it is really surprising to find how
flat the trajectory of his genius is, how little
he has declined from this its culmination. I
have myself heard "Love is Enough" criticised
in the statement that "Love is n't enough"; but
this is a clear *ignoratio elenchi*. The transla-
tions, prose and verse, have perhaps attracted
more unfavorable criticism than any other part
of the work; and although I am not competent
to decide whether Mr. Morris's sagas are or are
not unfaithful to their original, I can most
frankly admit that Mr. Morris's "Æneid" is
not exactly Virgil, and Mr. Morris's "Odyssey"
still less exactly Homer. But it really seems
unnecessary to fight over again the endless
battle of Translation *v.* Original. The translation is never the original, and Mr. Morris's sub-
stitutes are a great deal better than most. But
"Sigurd," at a time of life when the poetic tide
often runs low in a man, showed that Mr. Morris
was as good at practically original work as ever.
Indeed, I hardly know another instance of a

13

poet well advanced in years, if not old, who attempted a new and very dangerous metre with such extraordinary success. Once get the secret of this cunning mixture of anapæsts and trochees, and the varying and voluble melody of it will simply amaze you.

The last collection of poems proper, " Songs by the Way," contains chiefly gleanings of older years ; and with many delightful things (especially the incomparable " Meeting in Winter ") includes a good deal of Mr. Morris's very Colonel-Newcome-like politics. But a few years ago the indefatigable poet entered on a new course. It must be admitted that the most ingeniously perverse undergraduate could not have selected anything more likely to " disgust the examiners" than the types, etc., of " The House of the Wolfings." Whenever — which is often — I have a mind to read over the " Wood Sun's " perfectly exquisite forecast of Thiodulf's fate, — the best piece of English poetry published for these ten years past except " Crossing the Bar," — I have to lay my account with a pair of smarting eyes for the rest of the evening. But in this, and in "The Roots of the Mountains," and most of all in "The Glittering Plain," we have what before Mr. Morris even Kingsley never quite achieved, true sagas, not in the least mosaics or *pastiches* from the sagas proper, but "sets" or "cuttings" from them, instinct with genuine life, and reproducing with due variation the character of the parent stock.

In other words, we have in Mr. Morris what we have not had since Chaucer, and what no other nation has had since a time older than Chaucer's, a real *trouvère* of the first class — a person of inexhaustible fertility and power in weaving the verse and the prose of romance, and with a purely lyrical gift which even Chaucer did not often show. It is the quality of poetry — much more than the particular forms or the agreeable volume in which it manifests itself — that has always attracted me, and attracts me now as much as ever to this very remarkable writer. The quality of poetry is apt to be, if not strained, drowned when it comes to be written by the ten, the fifty, the

hundred thousand verses. I have made no
laboured calculation; but I really think that Mr.
Morris cannot be very far off, if he has not
actually reached or passed, the hundred thousand limit. He cannot be said to be quite free
from the faults of such prolixity, the loose
fluent phrase, the easy amble of movement,
the watered and undistinguished description.
And yet you shall never read many pages,
seldom many lines of his, without finding side by
side with these negligences the unmistakable
marks which a poet, and only a poet, impresses
on his work. From "The Defence of Guinevere" to the snatches in his latest prose works
he has these marks, in phrase, in music, in suggestion. And still, charming as are many of
the detached pieces to be culled from him,
the atmosphere and the tenor of the whole
seem to me to be more poetical than any of the
parts. All over it is that "making the common
as though it were not common" which is the
best if not the only existing definition of this
indefinable quality.

So, when I see in the work of certain writers

whom it is unnecessary to name, and whom I
do not allude to otherwise than for the sake
of honour, the falling back on strained expression, on flashes of poetical epigram and conun-
drum, on scrambles after the grand style and
fumblings after the marmoreal, I turn with relief
once more to the lambent easy light, the misty
lunar atmosphere shot with faint auroral colours, the low and magical music, the ever-vary-
ing panorama of poetical description and passion and thought that I have known so long,
and loved so much, in the writings of the author
of " The Earthly Paradise."

XXI.

MR. RUSKIN.

AFTER the havoc that has been made during the last four or five years in the ranks of the great seniors of English Literature there is, perhaps, but one name left, if indeed there be one, who shares the first class, in merit and seniority combined, with that of Mr. Ruskin. There is certainly none which has seen, during the lifetime of its owner, such curious vicissitudes of popular repute. It will soon be, if it is not already, fifty years since "A Graduate of Oxford" arose to admonish the British nation of its sins and shortcomings in the matter of art and appreciation of art. For some ten years or more after that, Mr. Ruskin was a voice crying in the wilderness, but attracting more and more younger voices to go and cry after him. For about twenty subsequent to this first decade he was a power, in some of his innumerable lines sweeping public taste more or less with or before him. And then the inevitable reaction which generally waits till after a man's death, but which in his case was hastened by certain oddities of his own whereon more must be said hereafter, set in with more than its usual severity. Young England, once Mr. Ruskin's disciple in art, has accomplished in regard to him the denial of St. Peter without St. Peter's repentance. It knows not the man; it will have none of him; it calls his favourite ideas "the Ruskinian heresy," and labours to set up some quite different thing from Ruskinism. And all the while, to those outsiders who can look coolly at the game, it is perfectly obvious that the blasphemers of Mr. Ruskin never could, metaphysically speaking, have come into existence but for Mr. Ruskin himself; and that they are, according to the well-known custom of certain savage tribes, eating their father.

I think I may speak without too great presumption for these outsiders. I have never been a Ruskinite, though I have always thought that nobody in our time has touched Mr. Ruskin at his very best as an artist in the *flamboyant* variety of English prose; and I have never been an anti-Ruskinite, though I know perfectly well what the anti-Ruskinites mean by their fault-finding, and even to a certain extent agree with it. When Mr. Ruskin began, as above remarked, to cry in the wilderness, it must be admitted by every one who gives himself the trouble to know, that he had a very great and terrible wilderness to cry in. I have never, being as has been said a hopeless outsider, been able to acquiesce in the stereotyped opinion (accepted docilely by a dozen generations of young would-be rebels) that Paris is an artistic Jerusalem, and London an artistic Samaria. But in the second quarter of this century we were in rather a bad way artistically. We had Turner (who was certainly a host, though a very undisciplined host, in himself), we had Etty (who has always seemed to me the prophet in art who has had least honour in this his own country), and we had

some others. But for sheer ugliness and lack
of artistic feeling in almost all respects, the reign
of William the Fourth and the first twenty
years or so of the reign of her present gracious
Majesty made what has been subsequently
termed a "record" in English history. Architecture had begun to feel a well-intentioned
but by no means always wisely directed revival;
music, painting, most sculpture, almost all
books, furniture, plate and domestic *supellex*
generally exhibited a perfectly hopeless level
of middle-class banality. I do not know that
matters have in all ways improved since.
With some things that are much better we
have had many things that are much worse.
We have had the vicious popularisation of cheap
machine-made art; we have had execrable vulgarities, we have had cant and affectation and
pastiche. But, whereas from the thirties to the
sixties, it was almost impossible to buy anything new that was not complacently hideous,
from the sixties to the nineties it has always
been possible to buy something new that was
at least graceful in intention.

And this was more the doing of Mr. Ruskin
than of any single man. Of course, nothing
of the kind is ever the doing of any single man.
The Oxford Movement, the Præ-Raphaelites,
the '51 Exhibition, — a horrid thing in itself,
— the increasing custom of travel abroad, and
a dozen other things not only helped, but did
much more than any man could do. But Mr.
Ruskin did as much as any man could do;
and that is a good deal. He had perfect
leisure, a considerable fortune, a wonderful
literary faculty, an intense love for art. He
was gifted by nature with what is the most
fortunate gift for a man of genius, the most
unfortunate for another, an entire freedom
from the malady of self-criticism. It has
never during his long career ever troubled Mr.
Ruskin to bethink himself whether he knew
what he was talking about, whether he was or
was not talking nonsense, whether he was or
was not contradicting flatly something that he
had said before. This is a great advantage
for a prophet in these or any times; and
Mr. Ruskin had it.

With such gifts he set himself to work to beat up the quarters of British Philistia, first in the department of art, and then in many another. At first he used Turner and the Præ-Raphael-ites for his battering-rams; then he was for a season wholly Venetian; then he spread himself widely into political economy and philosophis-ings of all kinds; then he erected a sort of private pulpit, and in "Fors Clavigera" and other things made almost a religion of his own idiosyncrasy; then, as all men know, he estab-lished himself at his own University and led men captive, as an irreverent one phrased it, by "road-making and rigmarole." Then a fresh band of Philistines, masquerading as the cir-cumcision of Art itself, set upon him and cried shame upon his version of æsthetics, and found fault with the imperfection of his technique, and urged Millet against Turner, and flung studio jargon against lecture-room mysticism. And meanwhile, oddly enough, his despised, and I must say I think rather despicable, Political Economy won the ground that his æsthetics had lost; and all or half of our socialists and semi-socialists nowadays talk "Unto this Last," without its mysticism or its eloquence, and with twice its unreason.

A most odd career: not exactly paralleled, so far as I can remember, and chequered by many things which in this rapid sketch I have had to leave out, such as the singular and very important relations of Mr. Ruskin to Carlyle. A career on which, no doubt, the anathema of the most distinguished of Mr. Ruskin's own Oxford contemporaries may be pronounced to the effect that it is "fantastic and lacks sanity"; which may be called (if anybody likes) a kind of failure; but which has influenced England in a vast number of different ways as the career of no other man living or lately dead has influenced it.

It is extremely difficult to criticise Mr. Ruskin, if only for the very simple reason that, as has been remarked already, he has never condescended to criticise himself. He once characteristically boasted that he "had never withdrawn a sentence, written since 1860, as erroneous in principle." In 1860 Mr. Ruskin was nearly forty, and we are to suppose (which, indeed, is self-evident from the complete re-casting of the earlier volumes of " Modern Painters ") that there was a good deal to with-draw before that. But the fact is that, dis-owned or not disowned, all his work in reality bears the same marks, — an intense love of beauty; a restless desire to theorise on beauti-ful objects; a vivid imagination; a rather weak logical gift; a strong but capricious moral sense; a knack of succumbing to any tempting current theory; a marvellous command of eloquent prose; and, as must be constantly repeated, an utter absence of critical faculty properly so called.

Such a combination with such faculties of expressing it must needs produce work as dis-concerting as it is stimulating. In his inequal-ities of style Mr. Ruskin is very much at one with all practitioners of prose during this cent-ury, and with most during others. But where he is almost unique is in his inequalities of thought and matter. Landor, who is his most easily suggested analogue in this, is not really

a parallel: for Landor's thought is never good
for much, it is at best not contemptible, and
presents a decent standard tradition from the
classics. Mr. Ruskin's is, for the most part,
purely original (with the suggestions and adop-
tions above noted), and at times it has really
marvellous vigour, felicity, and truth.   At
others, and just as often, it borders on sheer
nonsense.   It is customary to sneer at the
mystico-allegorical theology and philosophy of
the Middle Ages. But those who sneer forget that the men of the Schools were justified by the simple and massive theory that
their scheme of divinity, cosmology and an-
thropology was eternally and unavoidably true,
and that everything not merely might, but
must, be brought into harmony with it. Mr.
Ruskin's standards, on the other hand, are often
mere " will-worship," ideas which he has casu-
ally picked up in the state of hypothesis from
other men, and which he erects into eternal
truths.

He has, for instance, been reading Mr. Max
Müller, and he promptly reels off that mar-

vellous compound of ingenuity and folly, " The
Queen of the Air." He has been reading
somebody else, and he produces that astonishing mixture of namby-pamby guess-work and
suggestive thought entitled " The Ethics of
the Dust." Although he is scarcely ever
wrong in admiration, his dislikes are so capricious and so unreasonable, that one is almost
safe in saying, "When Mr. Ruskin passes
from praise to blame he may, as a rule, be
neglected." Nothing is too wild for him to
say when he is in his altitudes, and he will
gravely propose that certain goods, such as
coals and petroleum, shall be sent about only
by canal traffic, and the canal boats only towed
by men, because " it cannot matter whether
they get to their destination sooner or later."
He forgets, of course, or rather disdains to consider, first, that in certain circumstances men
won't tow ; and, secondly, that if some coals or
petroleum get to their destination slower than
other petroleum or coals, they will sell for less
money or not sell at all. Although the youngest
school which finds most fault with him has not,

I think, much *locus standi* for objecting to him,
as whimsical and one-sided, he is himself undoubtedly compact of whim, and it would not
need the courage of a Euclid to define him
as "a body with one side only." A crotcheteer
with a tongue of gold; an enthusiastic lover of
art who systematically ignores some of the first
laws of the artist; a political economist who
would bankrupt Eldorado and unsettle Sparta;
a moralist who does not know the meaning of
fairness; and a critic who does not know the
meaning of balance, — such is Mr. Ruskin.

XXII.

MR. RUSKIN (*concluded*).

ENOUGH must have been said in the last
paper of the singular weaknesses and
contradictions which meet us everywhere in
Mr. Ruskin. It remains to say something of
their probable causes, and of the merits which
accompany, and, as I think, far outweigh them,
everywhere but in his dabblings with economics.

The sources of Mr. Ruskin's peculiarities,
both in merit and defect, appear to me to have
lain as usual in his nature, and to have been developed as usual by his education. This latter
(as in the case of that other eccentric Camber-
well man, Mr. Browning) was of a home-keep-
ing and haphazard kind, very different from the
usual up-bringing of well-to-do middle-class
youth in England. It is true that Mr. Ruskin,
unlike Mr. Browning, went to a University,
though, like him, he went to no school; and

his comparative chastity of form may be partly
ascribed to this frequentation of the Muses.
But Christ Church, which does not like to be
called a " college " at all, is even now probably
the college of both Universities in which the
University and, strictly speaking, collegiate influences are weakest; while for a gentleman-
commoner in Mr. Ruskin's time they were
weaker still. The shaping, moulding, training
influence of the ordinary English liberal education has been abused as well as lauded, and
I suppose that it may to a certain extent and
in certain cases act as a cramp and a restraint;
but it certainly acts in a far greater number as
a beneficial discipline. Discipline is what Mr.
Ruskin has always lacked; as well in methods of
expression as in the serene self-confidence which
has enabled him to deliver himself on any and
every subject, without any suspicion that he is
talking ill-informed nonsense. Discipline Oxford did not give, had indeed no full opportunity
of giving, to Mr. Ruskin; but she gave him,
there can be no doubt, additional inspiration.
She nourished in him that passion for architec-

ture which no single city in the United King-
dom is so richly dowered with the means of
exciting and gratifying; and she, no doubt,
also strengthened in him the general Romantic
tendency of which he is so characteristic an
exponent.

For the other part of the matter it has long
ago seemed to me — I do not know that I have
seen it noticed or suggested by anybody else —
that the central peculiarity of Mr. Ruskin is a
singular and almost unparalleled union of two
main characteristics, one of which is usually
thought of as specially French, the other as
specially English. The first is an irresistible
and all-pervading tendency to generalize, — to
bring things under what, at any rate, seems
a law, to erect schemes, and deduce, and con-
nect. The other is the unconquerable ethical
tone of all his speculations. To follow out the
ramifications of this strangely crossed nature
of his would take a very great deal of space,
and would partake more of the style of abstract
criticism than would perhaps be suitable to this
book and plan. But one or two applications

and corollaries of what has just been said may
be indicated.

Thus it may be pointed out that Mr. Ruskin's
extraordinary insensibility to the ludicrous
hangs on to both the un-English and the English
sides of his intellectual temperament.   His
mania for generalizing blinds him to the absurd on the one side, as we constantly find
it doing in Continental thinkers; his insa-
tiable appetite for moral applications, and his
firm belief in his moral mission blind him, as
we find these things do often in Britons.   When
Mr. Ruskin says that a square leaf on any tree
would be ugly, being a violation of the law
of growth in trees, we feel at once that we are
in the company of an intellectual kinsman of
the learned persons whom Molière satirised.
He deprecates expenditure on plate and jewels
(while admitting that " noble art may occasion-
ally exist in these ") because they are matters
of ostentation, a temptation to the dishonest, and
so on, — a moral paralogism which would be
almost impossible to any one not of British
blood.

But I must leave this key to Mr. Ruskin in the hands of the ingenious reader, who will find it do a great deal of unlocking. A man with an ardent sense of duty combined with an ardent desire to do good; eager to throw everything into the form of a general law, but eager also to give that general law, directly or indirectly, mystically or simply, an ethical bearing and interpretation; extremely fond of throwing his discourse into an apparently argumentative form, but probably more prone than any man of equal talents who has lived during this century to logical fallacies and illicit processes of every kind, — grasp the man as this, and the works will cease to be a puzzle or an irritation, because the reason of them will at once be plain.

And it would be a very great pity, indeed, if the Book of Ruskin were to remain to any one merely a closed book, as irritation or as puzzle. For, if these curious volumes are taken with a due amount of rational salt, they cannot fail to enlarge and exercise the tastes and powers of the reader; while, if read simply for enjoyment, they will be found to contain the very finest prose (without exception and beyond comparison) which has been written in English during the last half of the nineteeth century. The great merit of this prose is that it is never, as most of the ornate prose styles of a more recent day are, affected and unnatural. Great pains have been spent on the writing of English prose during the last twenty years — greater, I think, than had been taken for several generations. But the result has almost always had (to my taste at least) something too much of the lamp — a too constant reminder that here the gentleman did take great pains, that he turned the sentence this way and that to convey an air of distinction, that he picked his words so as to give them, if not quite a new meaning and collocation, at any rate a collocation and meaning as different as possible from that which they had usually had. One thinks far too often of the story of Paul de Saint-Victor (a real artist, too) scattering single words about a paper, and then filling in and writing up to them. Our latter-day prose of this kind is sometimes eloquent, but it is rarely elegant; it is sometimes splendid, but it is seldom or never at ease; it is often quaint and rare in embellishment, but it is seldom or never unconscious of its dress.

Now, Mr. Ruskin's purple patches — despite a rather too great tendency to run not merely into definitely rhythmical, but into definitely metrical forms — are never laboured, they never suggest effort, strain, or trick. He warms to them naturally, he turns them out without taking his coat off. They are to be found, it is true, mainly, though by no means wholly, in his earlier books. The practice of alternately chatting and scolding, to which he unfortunately betook himself some five-and-twenty years ago, is not favourable to the production of fine English, unless the writer can rise to the level of a real *sæva indignatio*. This Mr. Ruskin can seldom do ; and, as has been already noted, his weaknesses never betray themselves so much as when he is talking of what he does not like.

But in his early days of enthusiasm he was often magnificent — no lesser word will do. It was some time before I could bring myself (well knowing what the comparative result would be) to compare the second of the two recent volumes of selections, which cover his whole work, with the early and now precious volume which was published in 1861, and which was perforce confined to the greater and earlier books— the " Modern Painters," the " Stones of Venice," the " Seven Lamps," the " Lectures on Architecture and Painting," and a very few others. In this older volume you will, no doubt, find the crochet and the waywardness, the para-logism and the undue preaching, not, as he once put it, of " the connection between art and human passion" (which is perfectly true and important), but of that between art and its influence on the life of the artist (which is chiefly not to the point). But you will also find far more frequently than later — indeed, in this volume on almost every page — a phras-ing so admirable, a selection of imagery so fertile and felicitous as to compel admiration, even if the matter, instead of being almost always noble (if not always quite sane), were purely wrongheaded or purely unimportant.

For more than forty years artists in flamboyant prose have been writing after and after the famous description of the Falls of Schaffhausen in "Modern Painters." Mr. Swinburne, in his "Blake," once very nearly, if not quite, equalled it; all the rest are nowhere. The "Stones of Venice" is crammed with similar passages; in fact, it is *the* book of descriptive prose in English, and all others toil after it in vain.

For happier expressions of crotchety fancy, where shall we look than in the rather numerous passages where Mr. Ruskin sets forth his favourite craze that bright colours are virtuous, dark and neutral tints wicked? The thing is false, it is almost silly; but it is so charmingly put that you chuckle at once with keen pleasure and mild scorn. Also, the man can observe, which is the most uncommon of all gifts. The fault of our modern impressionists lies in just this — that the artist seems to think he must empty out of his representation everything but the mere individual impression itself, so that he does not really give what he sees, or what anybody sees, but what is or might be seen with an arbitrary subtraction of allowance for the seer's presumed idiosyncrasy. This is as bad as the most slavish convention or the most exaggerated personal crotchet. Now, Mr. Ruskin certainly does not minimise the personal element; yet he can, when he chooses, keep it to its lowest terms.

But I am outrunning my limits. To sum up the impression side of the matter, — when I was young, Mr. Ruskin's crotchets used to irritate me more than they ought; they now irritate me hardly at all, and only bore me a little. But I think I like his beauties more than ever; and I am disposed to think, also, that he has brought more folk to art than he has ever bitten with his own heresies about it.

THE END.